"Kris Boesch as a CEO had 40% lower turnover than her competitors because she put joy first. By highlighting the right levers to make positive culture a choice, this book will walk ~~~ ~ ~~~ ~~~ ~~~ conversations to a full blown positive work worthwhile."

—**Shawn** ⟋
of *The Happiness*

"There are so many valuable nuggets in Kris's book—practical ideas from a leader who actually put them to work successfully scaling a company in a tough industry."

—**Verne Harnish,** author of *Scaling Up (Rockefeller Habits 2.0)* and founder Entrepreneurs' Organization (EO)

"*Culture Works* is a solid guide full of energy, humor and most importantly, practical advice. Improve your workplace culture, honor your employees as well as your mission, and sleep better at night— knowing you have a thriving team firing on all cylinders."

—**Marshall Goldsmith,** one of the top ten Most-Influential Business Thinkers in the World

"A helpful guide to developing and living your company's core values."

—**Tony Hsieh,** CEO of Zappos.com and author of *Delivering Happiness*

"Creating an intentional culture in today's business climate can be one of the most powerful forces for good. For our people, our communities, and our world. If you're serious about this, *Culture Works* will serve as a wonderful guide."

—**Kent Thiry,** CEO of DaVita Healthcare Partners

"This book shows you how to build a positive culture of happy, inspired people who bring commitment and motivation to their work."

—**Brian Tracy,** author of *Full Engagement*

"Whether you're a small company CEO or big company manager *Culture Works* is packed with leadership value bombs. This will go down as one of the best business books of 2017."

—**Kevin Kruse,** New York Times bestselling author
and founder of LEADx

Kris writes from the heart so you can lead from the heart. Improve your business AND be a positive influence in the lives of those you lead. Read *Culture Works* and learn to lead with joy.

—**Nancy Greatrix Manley,** Human Resource Director Room & Board

"Workplace culture is at the heart of business success. Kris has written the quintessential practical guide to securing profitability by creating an extraordinary culture."

—**Dr. Diane Hamilton,** MBA Program Chair for Forbes
School of Business and leadership expert, author and speaker

"*Culture Works* is the new must-have resource for recruiting, hiring, training and retaining employees who will not only sync with your team and your mission, but thrive and contribute for a very long time. Do your bottom line a favor and buy this book now."

—**David Kolb,** President of GTN, a mobility tax services firm

"Culture works for you or against you, but it is never silent. Using the practical advice in *Culture Works,* we reinforced our best habits, stomped out the bad ones, and aligned our whole company to her 'same team' approach. In a short time, we reduced turnover and found an army of engaged and motivated employees already in place just waving their arms and wanting to do more to move us forward."

—**Troy Lerner,** CEO at Booyah Advertising

"Lots of business books talk about workplace culture. *Culture Works* teaches you what to do about it! Kris Boesch provides an indispensable tool to focus on the people, process, and profit issues that face all businesses in today' s competitive environment. Her insights have transformed our company into a leader in our field and example of an employer of choice!"

—**Steve Pottenger,** CEO of Workwell Occupational Medicine

"This book is fantastic! I really appreciated all of the 'meat and potatoes' —rare these days to find in business books. And I loved the humor and real life business examples used throughout. I literally devoured it. There were also many sections and concepts I'll apply to personal life as well, making it doubly impactful."

—Jim Finnegan, Regional General Manager of Stout Street Hospitality

"Culture Works is the rare book that will get you to think and inspire you to act. Boesch makes a strong, science-based case for rethinking culture—and then provides the tools you need to transform your organization."

—Susan Grutzmacher, Division Director of Boulder County Community Support

"In *Culture Works* Kris Boesch has hit the nail on the head. As an entrepreneur, financial author, and big believer in employee accountability and financial transparency in an organization, this book is a valuable handbook and resource to people like me. As a finance guy I want to give Kris big kudos for estimating ROI on creating a happy and engaging workplace. I know businesses will be more profitable if they follow the principles in this book."

—Joe Knight, author of *Financial Intelligence* and partner of the Business Literacy Institute

"This is business, done right. This is the gentle addressing of a fundamental lack in the modern workplace: Joy. Thank you for this wonderful book."

—Tyler Knott Gregson, author of nationally best selling *Chasers of the Light*

culture
works

How to Create Happiness
in the Workplace

Kris Boesch

ISBN 978-0-9986711-3-0 (hard cover)
ISBN 978-0-9986711-2-3 (soft cover)
ISBN 978-0-9986711-4-7 (e-book)

First Kalina Publishing hardcover edition April 2017

For information about special discounts for bulk purchases, please send requests to cultureworks@choosepeople.com.

If you are interested in having Kris Boesch present at your live event or conference, visit www.krisboesch.com or e-mail kris@choosepeople.com.

Editing and copyediting by Jim Morrison
Cover design by Ivan Kurylenko
Interior design by Toolbox Creative
Illustrations by Alex Seciu

Kalina Publishing Inc.
Denver, CO

"When people feel good about coming to work it ripples into the community, into the homes and the coffee shops and the parks and ball fields. When people are happy at work, they are better parents, spouses, volunteers and citizens. When we make the workplace better, we make the world better."

Kris Boesch

To all the bosses, leaders, and managers
striving to do the right thing.

Contents

Chapter 4
Marshal Meaning, Momentum and Money

Chapter 5
Strengthen Shared Identity and Interdependency

Chapter 6
Shift Accountability

Chapter 10
Create Culture Conducive to Change

Chapter 11
Expand Time and Boost Focus

Chapter 12
Make Meetings Meaningful

Chapter 13
Implement Meaningful Performance Reviews—The Triad

Chapter 14
Crack the Compensation Code

Introduction

Do you feel joy when you walk into your workplace? Does your team?

I am talking about true joy, real happiness, too often a rarity in today's dysfunctional workplaces.

Over the past decade, I've researched and tested—in a variety of workplaces—concepts and tools to build a foundation of happiness that not only puts smiles on faces, but brings joy to your bottom line.

My journey to happy workplaces began out of the sheer need to survive. I was the newly appointed CEO of a moving company that on the surface seemed to be going places but behind closed doors was spiraling out of control. When you walked through the door tension fouled the air.

The shop was paralyzed, held captive by constant conflict. Gossip undermined communication. There was little trust. The crew hated management and management didn't have faith in the crew. Team members hurled obscenities at one another daily. In a nutshell, everybody was unhappy, unproductive and disruptive.

Our customers sometimes bore the brunt of unhappy movers who didn't care about their job much less the family's precious belongings. Our expensive moving equipment was left behind on jobs, walls and furniture were dinged and dented, and we were hemorrhaging money, struggling to make payroll.

I was the boss and I sure as hell didn't feel good about coming to work. Neither did my team.

It was a mess.

Press fast forward to a few years later and our company of frustrated misfits had transformed into a leader in the moving industry:

We had **40 percent less turnover and twice the profits** of the industry average.

A jaw-dropping turn around. How did we do it?

We learned the happy dance together, one step at a time. Of course along the way we stumbled, tripped and adjusted.

My experiences at the moving company led me to work with the Industrial Organizational Psychology department at Colorado State University a few years later. *There we discovered what makes employees feel good about coming to work—and how to measure it.* It's then that I opened the doors to my culture consultancy, Choose People. The tools outlined throughout this book are the result of my experiences backed by solid academic research.

I am a stand for joy in the workplace.

Shifting the national work conversation from one of apathy and woe to one of success through joy creates a ripple effect in our lives and in our communities.

When we make workplaces better, we make the world better.

Good news, it's not that hard.

What you hold in your hands is a how-to book. It's filled with juicy content and a lot of implementable "Action Jacksons." You can read it cover to cover. Or you can use it as a companion to the Culture Works workbook and book club, creating change chapter-by-chapter. The choice is yours how you use it; either way I'm glad you're along for the ride.

So...grab my hand and let's dance together into a more productive, a more profitable and a happier workplace.

Chapter 1

Measure Your Culture's Happiness

- Take the Litmus Test

- Master Your Organizational Triangle

- Choose Satisfaction, Engagement or Happiness

- What is Workplace Culture?

- Why Emotional Intimacy?

- Rock Newton's Cradle

- What Elephants?

- Measure Eight Critical Happiness Factors

- Complete The Diagnostic Survey

*"The measure of my success is the measure of
my happiness."*

—William John Locke, novelist and playwright

Before you waltz on to the dance floor, step back and learn where you are now. Find your starting place with this litmus test. It's as easy as the two-step.

Take the Litmus Test

Quickly, from the gut, answer, on a scale of 1–10, how happy are your employees? (Happy is defined as your employees feel good about coming to work.)

Write your answer here: _____

Now, before you go to the next page, jot some notes down about why you answered the way you did. Why not higher? Why not lower?

_____

_____

_____

_____

_____

_____

_____

_____

_____

_____

_____

_____

_____

_____

_____

_____

_____

Did you say 7?

When I ask CEOs, executive directors and deans to answer this question, most answer seven.

Seven is an interesting number. It's representative of "we're doing okay, not great," or "I really don't know." You're confident no one is going to go postal. Overall you have a good group of people who get along well enough. There are some areas that could use improvement. It's a "safe" number.

Very few answer five or less. If you answered six, chances are there are a few elephants tromping around your office. If you answered five or less, they're pregnant.

If you answered eight or above, congratulations! Chances are you feel pretty good about coming to work and overall feel like you have an organization where smiles are real, laughter is genuine and you can feel vibrant energy.

If you answered 10, then you know. You know what it takes to have an extraordinary workplace culture. Consistent attention, nurturing and learning. While there may not be as many big juicy "ah ha's" in this book for you, I'm confident you will find several nuggets to add to your repertoire.

Note: The number you selected is your perception. Unless you've actually measured your employees' happiness (yes this is doable—more to come), it's what you THINK your employees feel. You may be right. You may be wrong.

Don't despair if your number is low. Before I focused on culture, the moving company I walked into was a four on a good day.

Master Your Organizational Triangle

"You're a moron!"

"You're the dumbass!"

Those are a few of the kinder comments I heard in my first few weeks after arriving at the moving company. The crew cursed one another. Cash flowed slower than the obscenities. I was robbing Peter *and* Paul to cover payroll. I didn't have time and I didn't have money.

I needed a solution. Fast. I read business books, found mentors, sought advice and over time clarity emerged:

It all starts with my crew. If the crew feels good about coming to work, they'll take better care of our customers who in turn will feed the financial health of the organization.

Most work conversations are about your employees, your customers or your financials. All other elements fall under the umbrella of business strategy, product/service mix, and value proposition.

Many companies focus on financial health. Just the numbers, please. Clearly, if you don't have a financially sustainable organization you can't serve your clients nor pay your employees. However, financial health is a lag indicator. It tells you how you did, not what you need to do to get there.

It's also no wonder why organizations concentrate on their clients. They focus on retaining and growing their current base, prospecting for new ones, increasing word of mouth and providing exceptional customer service.

But, think about it. Who retains your current clients? Who provides that exceptional customer service? Who creates an experience for your customers worthy of generating word of mouth? Your employees!

The numbers don't create the numbers. Your people do.

Assuming you already have a proven business model, the ONE lever you can pull to significantly boost your financials is to improve the workplace experience of your employees. If your people feel good about coming to work, they will take good care of your customers, who in turn will support your bottom line.

My crew guys weren't just the face of my moving company. Heck, they WERE the company. They lugged the piano up the switchback staircase. They apologized and promised to follow through if something broke. They made our customers happy—the customers who became ambassadors by referring new clients—generating sustainable financial success.

I started to focus on my employees' daily experience at work. While moving isn't a "sexy" job, and some would suggest movers are a "difficult" workforce population, *in two years' time, we had 40 percent less turnover than the industry average and a bottom line twice that same average.*

How? Together we transformed our workplace culture.

Richard Branson, founder of the Virgin Group, nails this:

> "If the person who works at your company is 100 percent proud of the job they're doing, if you give them the tools to do a good job, [if] they're proud of the brand, if they were looked after, [and] if they're treated well, then they're gonna be smiling, they're gonna be happy, and therefore the customer will have a nice experience...
>
> So, my philosophy has always been, if you can put staff first, your customer second and shareholders third, effectively, in the end, the shareholders do well, the customers do better, and yourself are happy."

Choose Satisfaction, Engagement or Happiness

What's the most vital culture measurement for your organization?

Take a second and think with me. "Employee satisfaction" and "employee engagement" are problematic. A satisfied, unengaged employee is expensive, and an unsatisfied, engaged employee is potentially dangerous.

Satisfied is a lackluster low bar. If you ask your clients about your organization, how would you feel if they responded "satisfied"? Blah. "Engaged" is odd. No one says they want their kids to grow up and be "engaged"—married perhaps—but not engaged. Parents want their children to grow up and be happy. While your employees are not your children, happy is a real-deal, visceral emotion. You know what happy feels like. You know what happy looks like. You can literally experience someone else's joy. Remember the last time you heard an unabashed giggle.

Sometimes I get pushback, "But Kris, you can't *make* someone happy." I agree, you can't. What you can do is create a workplace that fosters joy. You can create the context and conditions that build happiness. Imagine, your morning starts out rough. Your beloved ate the last bagel. Rex chewed your new shoes. Traffic was brutal. Yet, when you walk through the front door of your organization you're transformed. You take a deep breath. You take that breath because you have just entered a place where the smiles are real, the laughter is genuine and you can feel vibrant energy in the room. It's magical.

OR you enter the front door, choke on oppressive air, stomach churning with anxiety.

I also hear, but Kris, "You can't have *everyone* be happy."
Again, I agree. I'm not asking everyone to be happy. I'm asking you to have a workplace environment where those *who are a good culture fit* can flourish. Happily.

Forget trying to make everyone happy. It's not possible.

Also keep in mind, at a dinner party, no one is asking, "Are you satisfied at work?" "Are you engaged at work?" Because it's awkward. Instead they ask, "What do you do? Where do you work? How do you like it?" Do your employees light up in response, shrug or go off on a tirade? Do they see themselves at your organization for years to come or are they looking for something better?

Ask yourself, do your employees feel good about coming to work? What's their experience when they wake up and get ready for work? Is it a sense of purpose and warmth? Or one of procrastination and dread?

I ask these questions in all seriousness. Once when I shared with a client how we literally measure, "Do your employees feel good about coming to work?" She blinked, paused and slowly said, "That's interesting...because at my last job, there were days when I was driving to the office and I'd think, *I'd rather get in an accident than arrive to work.*"

Ooof. My jaw fell open in shock as her statement reverberated. "Seriously?" I asked. The tears that welled up in her eyes answered.

It was heartbreaking to think someone dreaded clocking in so much they'd prefer risking their life. It validated my belief about the power and importance of people feeling like they belong, that they matter and are known in their workplace.

What is Workplace Culture?

What's the vibe when *you* walk into your workplace?

Is it electric, refreshing, and buzzing? Or toxic, tension-filled, and gray? Disney or DMV?

Workplace culture is the context within which your people work. It's the air they breathe while running your marathon. It's the emotional health of your workplace. Too few organizations pay attention to how employees are—or should be—feeling. They don't realize emotions are central to culture.

Don't think it matters? It does. Sigal Barsade, Professor of Management at The Wharton School of Business at the University of Pennsylvania, and Olivia O'Neill, an assistant professor of management at the School of Business at George Mason University, have studied the emotional culture at corporations, an all-too-often ignored component of success.

"Emotional culture influences employee satisfaction, burnout, teamwork, and even hard measures such as financial performance and absenteeism," they write. "Countless empirical studies show the significant impact of emotions on how people perform on tasks, how engaged and creative they are, how committed they are to their organizations, and how they make decisions. Positive emotions are consistently associated with better performance, quality, and customer service—this holds true across roles and industries and at various organizational levels. On the flip side (with certain short-term exceptions), negative emotions such as group anger, sadness, fear, and the like usually lead to negative outcomes, including poor performance and high turnover."

Why Emotional Intimacy?

Emotional intimacy is the secret ingredient to the secret sauce of culture. It's the cinnamon in your chili, the chipotle in your fish taco sauce, the rhubarb in your coffee cake.

Emotional intimacy is the social super glue that creates camaraderie and synergy. It's beautiful, connected, related energy. We know what emotional intimacy looks like between friends, families and lovers, whether we're around a campfire, a kitchen table or simply holding hands. We know the difference between making love and having sex. Yet what about emotional intimacy in the workplace?

It's the contrast between making a difference through your work and just having a job.

Unfortunately, emotional intimacy isn't being talked about in the workplace. Authentic camaraderie and connection are happenstance rather than intentional.

How do you create that magical experience in your workplace—for you and your team?

That's what this book is about.

Rock Newton's Cradle

Back in the heyday of the 80s, Newton's cradle, depicted on the front cover of this book, occupied prime real estate on many executives' desks. It should make a comeback. This simple elegant toy illustrates invisible emotional energy transference and the power of momentum. Let me explain.

Culture is the unseen emotional energy that flows through your team. I see the balls representing a team of five individuals. The three balls in the middle magically do not move but are passively active. The ball on one end impacts the second, imperceptibly sending energy through balls three and four, becoming expressed in ball five, which returns that energy. In your organization, that energy could be enthusiasm, trust or commitment. Or that energy could be gossip, sadness, or apathy.

> "There are studies that have proven emotions are contagious. For centuries, researchers have studied the tendency for people to unconsciously and automatically mimic the emotional expressions of others, and in many cases actually feel the same feelings simply by exposure to emotions in social interactions. Studies have found that the mimicry of a frown or a smile or other kinds of emotional expression trigger reactions in our brains that cause us to interpret those expressions as our own feelings. Simply put, as a species, we are innately vulnerable to 'catching' other people's emotions."
>
> **—Sherrie Bourg Carter,** PhD, in *Psychology Today*

A healthy culture requires that everyone both recognize and own their role in cause and effect, impact and reaction, emotion and motion. Meanwhile, leadership has the challenging task of detecting this invisible emotional energy transference between team members and constantly bringing it to light.

We do not exist in a vacuum.

What Elephants?

People are complex. A group of people even more so. It's no surprise an organization has people challenges.

Earlier in this chapter I mentioned you might have a few elephants tromping around your office. Elephants are anything but subtle. They pretty much go where they please and do as they please. So how do you recognize one that's banging around in your organization?

Take this Short Assessment

Here are the top 25 challenges I've heard from CEOs, business owners and executive directors. Throughout this book I will provide ideas and tangible tools to address each of these. Circle those challenges that resonate:

1. I have employees who ask for a raise and haven't done anything to deserve it.

2. We work hard to please our employees, but they're never satisfied.

3. My employees think I'm lining my basement with gold.

4. I don't think my employees care about our organization.

5. When problems arise, no one steps up and takes responsibility.

6. My employees only do what's in their job description, nothing more.

7. Several of our incentive programs have backfired.

8. I have an employee who's a rainmaker/superstar and totally toxic.

9. We have in-fighting between groups, almost to the point of spitballs over cubicles.

10. We're a family—dysfunctions included.

11. Because of our financial instability, there's fear in the air.

12. Gossip is rampant.

13. Our employees hate change, even if it's what's best.

14. I'm amazed at the false rumors in our workplace.

15. We're divided into old school and new school and never the twain shall meet.

16. I've recently lost one of my best people and I shouldn't have.

17. I have to micromanage or nothing will get done correctly.

18. We're awful at getting reviews done on time or at all. Everyone hates them.

19. We've promoted fabulous producers into mediocre managers.

20. I just don't have the time to give people pats on the back.

21. I don't know how to acknowledge great work without a promotion or a raise.

22. I'm in leadership, and sometimes I'm the last to know when there's a problem.

23. We used to have an incredible culture and we've lost the magic.

24. It's so hard to find good talent anymore, yet my competition seems to.

25. We're growing so fast, it's hard to bring all the new employees into the fold.

When you look at the above, where do most of your challenges fall? If they fall between statements:

- 1–7: Entitlement, apathy, or lack of buy-in are tromping around.
- 8–15: Straight up drama has the herd causing havoc.
- 16–25: Leadership conundrums abound.

Throughout the course of this book, I will give you tools to address all of the above beasts.

Measure Eight Critical Happiness Factors

Remember, the litmus test from the first page is based on your personal perception not scientific fact. You might have a few elephants but you're not sure who they are or where they came from. Or...you still may be wondering, does our organization have a two-day cold or long-term cancer? Do we need to improve a little or start towards massive transformation? What you need is a more accurate measure of your organization's culture.

As I mentioned in the introduction, I spent an intensive year with a team from the Industrial Organizational Psychology Department at CSU prior to starting Choose People. Our goal was to construct and validate a diagnostic tool that could assess how employees feel about coming to work. We've condensed more than 1,000 hours of research into Eight Critical Factors. They serve as the foundation of the Choose People diagnostic survey.

These are the Eight Critical Factors:

1. **Supervisor.** Do your employees have positive perceptions of their supervisor?

2. **Co-workers.** Do your employees have positive perceptions of their co-workers?

3. **Meaning/Job Fit.** Do your employees feel the work they do is meaningful and worthwhile?

4. **Autonomy.** Are employees satisfied with the level of decision-making authority, control, and freedom they have in their work?

5. **Impact.** Do employees feel their work has an important role in the organization?

6. **Organizational Support.** Do employees feel the organization values, supports, and communicates appropriately with them?

7. **Organizational Fit.** Are employees connected to the organization? Is the organization a good match for them?

8. **Work-Family Climate.** Do employees feel the organization accommodates family needs and encourages a balance between work and family life?

(Please note, starting in chapter three, the factors most impacted by the chapter's content will be represented by the above icons.)

What is fascinating about this list is what is NOT included. Compensation, benefits and perks did not make it into the top eight. Based on our research, all eight of these factors are equally weighted. Meaning, in order to have a culture where your employees feel good about coming to work, all eight are equally important.

However, they are not all equally weighted for each individual on your team. You may have one employee who seethes if you micromanage them (autonomy is their priority) or another who needs to know they won't get the stinkeye upon returning from their kid's school registration (work-family climate is their priority). You need all eight together to meet the needs of your entire team and to create an extraordinary workplace culture.

The eight factors are about *perceptions and feelings,* that wonderfully intangible world of human experience and emotion. It can get a little messy, so it's understandable why many organizations struggle with culture.

Complete the Diagnostic Survey

Before you begin to address the elephants in your workplace, why not take a moment to measure how you feel about your workplace experience. To access your Culture Audit™ assessment, simply go to www.cultureworksbook.com, click on the button "Take Your Assessment" and answer the validation question. You will receive your results right away. The survey consists of 52 statements and takes an average of nine minutes to complete.

CAUTION: You may be tempted to duplicate this survey and give it to all of your employees because you're curious. You really want to know where your culture stands. I appreciate both the intention and the temptation. **Don't.**

Confidentiality and anonymity are mission critical to accurate results. So is participation. Your employees have to trust the survey provider and believe in the purpose for taking the survey. At Choose People **we have an extraordinary average response rate of 96 percent.** The average for most internal surveys is 33 percent.

This is also only the first discovery step we use in a five-step process to improve, shift and transform workplace cultures. YOU MUST take action on the results or your culture will be worse off for it. No one appreciates offering their thoughtful requested opinion only to have it ignored. Your people will be angry if they feel placated or if the actions fall to the wayside like last quarter's flavor of the month.

You can have your entire team take this survey, by contacting us at cultureworks@choosepeople.com.

You now know why happiness is a legitimate indicator of an extraordinary workplace culture and the role emotional intimacy plays in creating joy. Before we take next steps to bump up your litmus number, let me speak to the savvy financial voice in your head.

Chapter 2

Know the ROI of Happy Employees

- Is Your Employment Brand Costing You?
- Understand the True Costs of Culture
- Know the Financial ROI of Happy Employees
- Calculate Your Culture's ROI
- Recognize the Emotional ROI

"The most powerful and enduring brands are built from the heart. They are real and sustainable. Their foundations are stronger because they are built with the strength of the human spirit."

—Howard Schultz, CEO of Starbucks

Is Your Employment Brand Costing You?

What is your reputation in the talent marketplace?

If word on the street is that you churn and burn through people or that your organization is a soul-sucking place to work, your recruitment and retention challenges will continue. If you're known for genuinely caring about your people, talent will come to you.

Does your employment brand cost you? Or does it bring value to your doorstep?

Your culture determines your employment brand. Your employment brand controls your recruitment and retention efforts. Start with your culture and your employment brand will follow.

Here's why your organization's culture has to be phenomenal, now more than ever.

1. **Employees no longer feel trapped:** According to Gallup's 2017 poll, 50 percent of Americans say it is a good time to find a quality job (the highest level in 15 years). Talent now has options. Lots of options. "You're lucky to have a job" doesn't cut it. The recessional fear of ending up on the street facing grim prospects has markedly diminished.

2. **Higher turnover:** According to the 2013/2014 PWC Saratoga Practice Study, "Critical talent is leaving at a 20 percent higher rate than they were the year before. First-year turnover rose to 24.1 percent, the highest it has been since before the recession."

3. **Boomers are retiring:** 26 percent of the U.S. workforce consists of Baby Boomers. On average, 10,000 Baby Boomers (born between 1946–1964) retire every day. The U.S. Bureau of Labor Statistics predicts a shortfall of 5 million workers by 2020.

4. **Talent shortage:** 46 percent of U.S. employers currently have difficulty filling jobs due to lack of available talent per the ManPower Group 2016/2017 Talent Shortage Survey.

5. **Workplace culture is the most important recruitment factor:** LinkedIn's Talent Trends 2014 report noted that 60 percent of respondents said the most important factor when considering a new job was "the company has a reputation as a great place to work."

Retention and recruitment of your best people just got a lot more interesting.

Remember this: culture is a self-fulfilling cycle. The more effective your culture, the better your employment reputation and the easier it will be to retain and attract the right talent. But it all starts with employees who feel good about coming to your workplace.

Understand the True Costs of Culture

Perhaps you (or someone on your leadership team) feels you can't afford to have happy employees because you don't have the budget of Google or Apple.

There's a common misperception that to have happy employees you have to offer top-of-the-market compensation and dole out fabulous perks.

First, let's look at perks. A massage would be nice. So would a retreat in Hawaii. But, the value is temporary. If you come back from your relaxing lunch massage to sit down next to your vampire co-worker, the one you sit next to every day, all day, the massage might be just enough to keep you sane. Forget happy. Or if you return from Hawaii to toxic drama where none of your innovative ideas can see the light of day, the glow of your tan wears off, quickly. Perks often are nothing more than lipstick on a pig.

Second, let's look at pay. Remember that all-star employee you gave a substantial raise? The same one who shortly thereafter gave you notice and went elsewhere, maybe even to your competition for less pay? Compensation is important, but it's not even in the Top Eight Critical Factors to having employees feel good about coming to work.

Third, there are many ways you can create and keep happy employees that don't cost a dime. Stay tuned, more in the coming chapters.

Fourth, **you cannot afford NOT to have happy employees.** Why?

Know the Financial ROI of Happy Employees

Many business leaders believe culture is a "nice to have," rather than a financial necessity. They see it as the fluffy, sweet stuff. Wrong. This warm, fuzzy goodness supports cold hard cash.

I wasn't kidding when I said you can't afford NOT to have happy employees. Look at these numbers and then calculate your own.

CONSERVATIVE ANNUAL ESTIMATIONS

For an employee with an annual salary of $40,000
This chart is based on an employee
contributing twice their salary to revenues.

Estimated Cost of ONE Unhappy Employee	
10 percent less productive than an average employee	-$8,000
Emotionally contagious negativity (5 emps/1 hour/week @ $20/hour)	-$5,200
Bad customer service (25% admit to taking frustration out on customers)	-$2,500
Turnover—6 months of salary	-$20,000
More safety incidents	-$2,000
Harder to recruit (harm employment brand)	-$1,000
	-$38,700
Estimated Cost of TEN Unhappy Employees	-$387,000

Estimated Value of ONE Happy Employee	
12 percent more productive than an average employee	$9,600
Emotionally contagious joy (5 emps/1 hour/week @ $20/hour)	$5,200
14 percent better customer service and 89 percent better customer satisfaction rate	$2,500
Absent 41 percent less often than unhappy employees	$1,000
Fewer mistakes—26 percent fewer mistakes	$2,000
Easier to recruit (help employment brand)	$1,000
30–37 percent more successful with sales (if salespeople)	
	$21,300
Estimated Value of TEN Happy Employees	$213,000

Estimated Value of ONE Unhappy Employee *becoming* a Happy Employee	$60,000

For an unhappy salaried employee, you are looking at a bottom line impact of 1.5 times their salary—in this case, for a $40,000/year employee, a loss of $230/work day. Keep in mind that with an "average" indifferent employee, who is neither happy nor unhappy, you lose out adding a bottom line impact of half their salary.

Don't agree with these estimates? Here's a few of the statistics that support the above calculations:

1. The likelihood of job turnover at an organization with rich company culture is a mere 13.9 percent, whereas the probability of job turnover in poor company cultures is 48.4 percent.

   Source: Elizabeth Medina Columbia University study "Job Satisfaction and Employee Turnover Intention: What Does Organizational Culture Have to Do With It?"

2. Happy workers are 12 percent more productive than average while unhappy workers are 10 percent less productive than average (for a total spread of 22 percent!)

   Source: Andrew Oswald, Professor of Economics at Warwick Business School.

3. Employees in highly participative work climates provided 14 percent better customer service, committed 26 percent fewer clinical errors, demonstrated 79 percent lower burnout, and felt 61 percent lower likelihood of leaving the organization than employees in more authoritarian work climates.

   Source: Angermeier, Dunford, Boss & Boss; *Journal of Healthcare Management.*

(I don't want to bore you with all the stats, however if you want all the stats that support these calculations, just go to page 183 at the very end of this book.)

A few items to note about the ROI calculations:

- Researchers haven't quantified the financial impact of an emotionally negative employee, though we've all felt a meeting room go pallid due to an energy vampire. There is a flipside because we know of the employee who is an energy infuser. They're worth their weight in cupcakes.

- When it comes to the financial impact of a significant hit to your employment reputation, I think of two companies, one whose angry employee publicly posted on GlassDoor.com unsavory details that couldn't be easily removed and the other whose disgruntled employee texted vitriol and confidential information to the entire team successfully harming the organization.

- Costly recruitment becomes easier when happy employees share with their social circles how much they love where they work. Your employment brand gains significant magnetism to attract high level, prime culture fit talent.

- **26 percent fewer mistakes is amazing!** Think about your organization's last big mistake. Think about the pain: the loss of credibility, the loss of pride, the loss of focus, and the loss of momentum. Mistakes are great opportunities to learn, but in the moment, they're brutal. Imagine if you could reduce the number of mistakes made in your organization by 26 percent simply by having a better workplace culture.

Calculate Your Culture's ROI

Check out our "Ball Park Calculation" of the impact of your culture on your bottom line on our Choose People website at www.choosepeople .com/culture-calculator. You will need your total number of employees, average salary and your litmus test number.

Looking to One Day Sell Your Business?

One more financial consideration for those of you who are owners: when you're ready to sell your company, the buyer will be looking not only at the capacity of the individuals on your team, but also at the overall culture. Culture is an intangible asset that improves your bottom line and increases the sale price. So while you cannot monetize it as a separate asset, it creates leverage and confidence in negotiations. An extraordinary workplace culture and positive employment brand contribute to goodwill valuation.

Recognize the Emotional ROI

So, yes, the bottom line business case for having your employees feel good about coming to work seems to be a no-brainer. But let's take another slice at this—the emotional return on investment. Remember we measure whether your employees *feel good* about coming to work. (Almost makes me want to break out into a James Brown boogie.)

When people feel good about coming to work, they go home and show up as better parents, better spouses and better citizens. I don't know about you, but if I've had a crappy day at work and I arrive home, even my dog looks up at me and is like, "Uh, yeah mom, I'll just walk myself." It's hard to show up as your best self after a bad day. If I don't check myself, I'll be impatient and grumpy. We all have rough days, but it's another thing to experience a toxic, demoralizing work environment day in and day out.

When people feel good about coming to work, there's a ripple effect in our communities. When work is going well you enjoy your team, you know your contribution matters and your work is valued. Your sense of personal pride, confidence and dignity deepens. We become more present to others, leading us to be kinder, more helpful and more generous.

Imagine a household where the parents love where they work. Now imagine one where they hate it. Imagine their thoughts as they drive home. How they show up to their kids, their exchange with the neighbors. The weekends free time to create memories or paltry stress relief.

Now, imagine the single person, the young couple, and the empty nesters who love where they work. Now imagine one where they hate it.

How do you feel about coming to work? How does that impact how you show up at home?

In summary, your culture dramatically drives and impacts your profit. A better culture equals a better bottom line. As the width of your team's smiles expands, so does the impact of your mission.

Chapter 3

Fortify Your Foundation

- Author Your Mission: Warm Gooey Center

- Dream Your Vision: Your Three-Year Destination

- Illustrate Your Values: Reputation

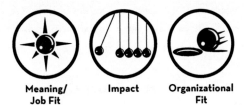

**Meaning/
Job Fit**   **Impact**   **Organizational
Fit**

"People don't buy what you do. They buy why you do it."

—Simon Sinek, marketing consultant and author of *Start With Why: How Great Leaders Inspire Everyone to Take Action*

Employees also buy *why*. According to Lindsay McGregor and Neel Doshi, co-founders of Vega Factor. "After surveying over 20,000 workers around the world, analyzing 50 major companies, conducting scores of experiments, and scouring the landscape of academic research in a range of disciplines, we came to one conclusion: *Why we work determines how well we work.*" Two of the ways your team assesses the factor of Organizational Fit is determining if they believe in your mission and if your values are similar to theirs.

Author a mission worth believing in, a vision worth working towards and values worth upholding.

Some of you may be thinking, "Oh no, not mission, vision and values again." Eyes glaze over, heads loll back and audible snores can be heard.

Plenty of business books cover this topic. There's a reason. It's important and foundational. I would be remiss if I didn't spend a few pages here suggesting that you exercise and eat better for your health. Just take into consideration Deloitte's Core Beliefs & Culture Survey that found employees who work for organizations with a strong sense of purpose are more confident in their organization's ability to deliver top quality products and service (65 percent) and focus on long-term sustainable growth (55 percent).

If you love your mission, vision and values and they resonate with your team, skip this chapter and head onwards and upwards. However if they're stale, you can't remember them or they feel "meh," read on.

Author Your Mission: Warm Gooey Center

Clearly explain how your organization makes the world a better place.

Think about a moving company. On the surface, its mission is to move belongings from A to B in good condition. While true, it's not inspiring. It's not inspiring because it doesn't speak to WHY and HOW belongings are moved.

When I held orientation with a new group of crew-members, I would tell them, "Moving is one of the most stressful experiences people go through. People are not their best selves when they're moving. They may also be dealing with the aftermath of a death or divorce. Then you come along and load all of their worldly possessions into your truck, and drive away. It's your job to provide peace of mind. It's your job to help people through one of the most difficult transitions in their life. Our customers need to know you care about their belongings and about their lives. Our tagline 'We Provide Peace of Mind, All in One Piece' isn't just a marketing slogan. It's what we do every day, all day."

It was amazing to watch many of these young men leave orientation with a peacock's pride, knowing their work was important. They were no longer in a second-class job, to be mumbled under their breath at the family picnic. Being a mover meant they were not only strong and hard-working, but they were helping people through one of the most difficult transitions of their life. In addition to creating pride, this awareness brought forth impressive empathy when caring for our customers. They went the extra mile because it mattered. Because they mattered.

People want to contribute. They want to achieve. They want to make a difference. Connect them to what matters.

Why does your organization exist in the world? Why do you do what you do? If you're a for-profit company, yes, you exist to make money. But your service or product does more than that and so does your team. Your organization brings joy, solves a problem, provides ease or saves time. So do your team members. Connect those dots for them.

Good companies do this. Medtronic sends its engineers out into the world to see the medical devices they've made in action so they can viscerally watch and feel the purpose of their work. UCB Pharmaceuticals invites patients to executive meetings so the people in charge can hear about their work making a difference. Every workday each DaVita employee housed at headquarters walks by a dialysis treatment chair on the way to their desk.

I was presenting the concept of connecting the dots to a CEO peer group when a man raised his hand and said, "While I appreciate the concept, we make inner tubes for tractor tires. Not exactly inspiring stuff. We're in manufacturing—we work all day in a plant where it smells, it's dirty and it's loud."

I looked at him and said, "Are you kidding? What you do is essential! If you didn't make the inner tubes for the tractor tires, then the tractor wouldn't work, and if the tractor didn't work, the fields wouldn't be plowed and the food wouldn't be harvested. Your inner tubes for tractor tires not only help support the success of farmers, they help feed and nourish our nation."

Your mission is your gooey center. It is the warm, beating heart of why you do what you do. It's why you contribute your life to this work and ask others to do the same. **Your purpose is your mission. Your mission is your purpose. It speaks to WHY you exist, what you stand for and it reflects your core ideology.**

 **Action Jackson:**
Uncover Your Mission

If you're struggling to come up with your mission, connect the dots. Keep asking "Why?" until you get to that **simple elegant nugget that's true.** Stop before it gets too existential or sounds like marketing propaganda. Start by watching Simon Sinek's TED Talk on "How Great Leaders Inspire Action (https://www.ted.com/talks/simon_sinek_how_great_leaders_inspire_action).

Please note, while your mission ideally aligns with your marketing and desired reputation, it is more important for your mission to resonate with your team than with your clientele.

You will know you have hit the jackpot when your simple phrase gives you goosebumps and resonates with your top performers. It's easy to understand and repeat.

To uncover your gooey center, consider answering the questions below. Note those words that "pop" the most. Your concise, simple mission statement should consist of a strong verb and simple, tangible language.

- What would be lost if our organization ceased to exist?
- Why does what we do matter?
- How do we contribute to society?
- What joy do we bring? And why?
- What pain do we solve? And why?

Then ask why three more times.

Dream Your Vision: Your Three-Year Destination

Time has gotten faster and attention spans shorter. Even more so if you're a smaller or newer organization. You need a measurable, attainable vision, one everyone can imagine three years from now.

Why three years? It's far enough ahead to achieve significant strides, but not so far ahead it lands in the dreamy "some day, one day" realm of unreachability. Another key consideration is most content employees envision themselves working for your organization for another three years. Part of what makes a vision successful is the team can imagine not only participating in making it a reality, but also crossing the finish line together and celebrating.

Your vision provides a single core focus. It is the ruler against which effort, progress and success is measured for the next three years. If you're serious, all of your strategic resources are organized around achieving this effort.

The biggest challenge with a vision is creating a reachable goal. It has to be worthy and winnable. Nothing is worse than feeling your team's eye rolls of "so what?" or "good luck with that."

Make sure to test it by asking—does it inspire us? Does it feel right? Does it sound like BS? Does it feel both possible and challenging?

How important is your vision? James Kouzes and Barry Posner, authors of *The Leadership Challenge*, surveyed thousands of workers worldwide and asked what they looked for in leaders and colleagues. In each case, number one was honesty. For leaders, number two by a wide margin—72 percent—was vision. Your team needs you to have a focused, attainable vision.

Choose People's Vision

Choose People's mission is to increase joy in the workplace. Our vision is to shift the national conversation around work from one of woe to one of joy.

The tipping point to have a conversation take hold is 12–14 percent of a target population. There are 126 million workers within the United States, 14 percent is 17,624,600 people. Luckily, others are also doing great work in this arena so we don't have to reach 17.6 million people by ourselves.

We will measure participation by book sales (thanks for helping!), keynote and workshop audiences, teams participating in our Culture Audit™ and Culture Tip subscribers.

Make it measurable and put a date and time on it. It's Monday, November 23, 2020, 5 pm MST and Choose People will have shifted the national conversation around work to one of joy for one million people.

You may be tempted to put a monetary amount in your vision. Or a market share. Or a number of units sold. Don't. Think through what it would take to get to that number. What's the one result, action or experience that would fulfill on your mission and create financial success?

Instead of "Within three years, we will dominate our industry," consider, "Within three years, we will solve the number-one customer frustration considered an industry norm."

For example, if you're an HVAC company, "We will eradicate the four-hour window and arrive at a set time." This competitive edge then allows the HVAC company to dominate the industry.

When defining the vision, a leader receives feedback and suggestions from the team, but at the end of the day, she has to make and own the decision. The leader is in charge of seeing the big picture daily and thus should have the widest view of the horizon and deepest sense of the implications for choosing one course of action vs. another.

Action Jackson:
Dusty Your Vision

To define your next vision, bring your core team together and brainstorm around the following questions:

We're sitting here in three years—

- What do we aspire to become, achieve, create? What do we want to be known for?

- Looking at our mission, what significant, realistic milestones would make us proud?

- Of these, which is most meaningful for fulfilling our mission?

- What does this milestone make possible?

- How will we measure success?

- Is this a reachable goal? Is it worthy and winnable?

- What does the organization look like and feel like if we're achieving this vision?

- Take a cue from Henry Ford's quote below. How can we anchor the emotional experience of what's possible for our team and for our clients when we achieve this vision?

  "I will build a motor car for the great multitude...it will be so low in price that no man making a good salary will be unable to own one and enjoy with his family the blessing of hours of pleasure in God's great open spaces...When I'm through, everybody will be able to afford one, and everyone will have one. The horse will have disappeared from our highways, the automobile will be taken for granted...and we will give a large number of men employment at good wages."

Illustrate Your Values: Your Reputation

Your values guide your decisions and thus your words, behaviors and actions. Your values, when followed, create your desired reputation.

From an organizational standpoint, values speak to a shared commitment, a communal identity. The daily experience of *how* you choose to fulfill the Mission and reach the Vision is rooted in your values. Values define both who gets to play on your playground and who doesn't. They signify not only what's expected, but also what's required. They set the bar for how you and your team are going to work together.

Aligned values are the fresh air your team breathes when they need to become grounded and focused, to find clarity when making hard decisions and to deal with a challenging client or co-worker.

Consider Zappos, the hugely-successful online retailer, where values are so important that a cultural fit interview is half the weight of whether a person is hired.

Action Jackson:
Uncover Your Values

To uncover your values consider the following:

- What do we stand for? What do we stand against?
- What values guide our decisions when making tough choices?
- What are we known for?

- What is our "way"?

- What values are highlighted in commonly shared stories?

- What are common phrases, ethos, behaviors and attitudes?

- What do these values look like in practice? How do we know if we're "living" the values?

Make sure to apply your organization's unique personality to your values. Values like "Respect" and "Integrity" are rudimentary basics to employment, essential and assumed.

Some of My Favorite Values:

- Chutzpah and Humility
- Assume Positive Intent
- Continuous Improvement
- Continuous Comfort Zone Expansion
- Fail Fast
- Grit, Perseverance and Resilience
- Be a Stand for one Another's Success
- Kind, Candid and Constructive Communication
- Play Big
- Progress over Perfectionism
- Expand Joy
- Courageous Curiosity
- Financial Freedom
- Do What's Right, Not What's Easy
- Champion Responsible Freedom
- Be Passionate and Pragmatic

Mission, vision and values are the foundation upon which a culture is grounded. Connect the dots, create goosebumps, define the direction, describe the destination and herald how you will work together.

Chapter 4

Marshal Meaning, Momentum and Money

- Quick Quiz: Are your Mission, Vision and Values Alive?

- Activate Mission, Vision and Values

- Plan the Strategic Work, Work the Strategic Plan

- Marry Money to the Mission

- Show Them the Money—The Invaluable $100 Tool

**Meaning/
Job Fit**

Autonomy

Impact

**Organizational
Fit**

"If you want to build a ship, don't herd people together to collect wood and don't assign them tasks and work, but rather teach them to long for the endless immensity of the sea."

—Antoine de Saint-Exupery, writer and pioneering aviator

Quick Quiz: Are your Mission, Vision and Values Alive?

You may have a thriving mission, vision and values. However for many organizations, those three pillars are not alive and well. They are a dusty, crumbling document in a filing cabinet of good intentions. Or worse, they're printed and posted, ridiculed for their hypocrisy, dead but not forgotten.

Take a moment and ask three of your team members if they know the organization's mission, vision and values. Before you do, though, and be honest here, and without looking, do you know them? If you don't, you have your answer. No need to ask anyone else.

Did your team look miffed? Or stutter and look away? Or come up with part of one and then their words trailed off? If so, it's time to bring them into the employment life cycle as well as into the organizational systems and processes.

Operationalize Values in Your Employment Cycle and Processes

Here's an extensive list. Read through the entire list and then go back through and evaluate three areas where your organization could most benefit from integration. Here's a clue: it's often where there's the biggest disconnect between the values and the current experience.

The Employment Cycle
Recruitment and Onboarding

- Your Employment Branding
- Job Posting
- Job Description
- Application Process
- Interviewing Process
- Hiring Process
- Orientation
- Training

Retention

- Performance Reviews
- Promotion Criteria

- Compensation Choices
- Appreciation and Recognition
- Professional Development
- Mentoring
- Co-Worker Camaraderie
- Character and Competency Correction
- Stay Interviews

Transition

- Dismissal Experience
- Turnover

Organizational Processes
Strategy

- Strategic Planning
- Goal Setting and Measurement
- Org Chart
- Research and Selection of Opportunities
- Creation of Product or Service
- Fulfillment on Product or Service

Communication

- Meetings
- Decision Making
- Celebration of Successes
- How Handle Mistakes
- How Handle Failure
- How Make, Save and Spend Money

Relationships and Reputation

- Marketing
- Sales
- Customer Service
- Accounting
- Vendor Relationships
- Competition Relations

Activate Mission, Vision and Values

Here are some examples of how you can take your mission, vision and values and operationalize them within your current processes and systems:

Under each value, describe what it looks like for an employee to embody that value. Here's a couple of examples from my stellar client SpatialKey:

- **Stand for one another's success.** We are dedicated to expanding the potential of our clients and our team.
  - Consider what's best for the organization, our clients and yourself
  - Say what needs to be said with kindness and candor
  - Do what's right, not what's easy
  - Witness and appreciate each other's contributions
- **Come from a place of courage.** We invent and embrace new ideas by approaching challenges with fresh eyes and curiosity.
  - Explore all possibilities
  - Question the status quo and ask, "What if?"
  - Respect your gut
  - Embrace thoughtful risk and expand your comfort zone
  - Be hungry, yet humble

Consider what your organizational structure would look like if it represented your values. For example, Wide Open West (WOW!) holds the value of "Servanthood: Embrace the attitude and honor of serving others rather than being served." Colleen Abdoulah, the former CEO of WOW!, implemented an inverted triangle hierarchy with customers on top, front line employees right below, then department managers and lastly leadership on the bottom. She saw leadership in a servant role, holding up the rest of the team.

Make it visible! Have your mission, vision and values thoughtfully printed, framed and posted. Post in the "about us" and "career" sections of your website. Consider putting them in your e-mail signature. Find some fun tchotchkes. Get fake tattoos, groovy coffee mugs, or office refrigerator magnets.

Include your values in the hiring process. Include them in every job description and job posting. Test for values alignment in behavioral interviewing and in reference checks. Ask the legal, uncomfortable questions. Turn down a well-qualified candidate because your gut says no. Turn down a less-than-qualified candidate even though you're desperate to reduce burnout of current staff. Tell your brother's belligerent son he can't work for you. Honor candidates you're not selecting with encouraging, timely communication.

Incorporate your values into the orientation experience. If you have Professionalism or Excellence as a value, are all of the resources and materials a new team member will need to be successful available their first week? Or does the desk still have sticky spots and crumbs on it from the prior employee? Think how you could welcome a new employee in a way that aligns with your values. Hazing? Balloons? Have leadership and team members share stories of how your organization has demonstrated its values and what it means to live your organization's "way."

Speak to what it means to be the face of your organization. Communicate clear expectations about job performance. Communicate clear expectations about character. For example, how they show up, interact with co-workers, or handle difficult situations. Communicate both what you stand for and what you're a stand against.

Ground new-hire training and trainer. Be clear on why the training is important, clarify how the skill being learned supports achieving the vision that fulfills on the mission. Question quarterly, "Is this training the best use of our time and energy resources when we consider the vision at hand?"

Keep in mind, we learn the most from the people who are closest in proximity. Peers matter most. A new person will turn to a co-worker at the desk next to him and repeatedly ask "on the job" questions. Make sure the go-to person is not only knowledgeable, patient and welcoming but representative of your values. Be strategic about providing mentors. New people can easily be lured by your most toxic team members. Toxic team members look for new allies and bond by sharing "insider" information (aka gossip), making new employees feel a sense of belonging.

Fire toxic people. One of the quickest ways you can demonstrate the "realness" of your mission, vision and values is by removing those individuals who are not a good culture fit. Note this is only after you have truly given them a chance to correct their character flaw. (See pages 67–72.)

Incorporate the values into performance reviews. What percentage of someone's employment in your organization is based on how well he embodies those values? Green Ride, an airport shuttle service company I worked with created a Character and Competency Performance Review (page 161) and declared that exemplifying their values consti- tuted 60 percent of someone's performance score. They were able to objectively evaluate the values alignment of a team member based on follow through of the top actions defined to live each value (regardless of whether they were a reservation agent, dispatcher or driver).

Use the Mission, Vision and Values as a touchstone to provide strategic clarity. Speak to all three at the beginning of key meetings. Have them be the container, the context, within which a strategic discussion is held. They should be at the forefront of all decision making, especially when accepting new initiatives and terminating others. Commitment to values at every turn helps a team navigate tough decisions with pride and integrity.

Implement bi-annual "Integrity Checks." Consider an informal brown bag lunch discussion. Ask, are we in alignment? Are we who we say we are? Do we have any new stories that demonstrate alignment?* Are there any stories we would like to add to our organization's canon? Do we have examples of where we fail to adhere to our values? Have we kept our energies and resources focused on the vision at hand? Or has a "shiny blinky" taken front stage? Or perhaps a crisis? How have we fulfilled our mission in the last six months? What are we proud of? Where are we struggling?

*In the days leading up to the discussion, encourage employees to think about stories not only from their teams, but from across the organization.

Take your values and have each department think through how to breathe life into them. For example, if one of your values is Transparency, here are some tangible actions that embody this value:

- Candid conversations are the norm.
- Share strategic decisions throughout the organization.
- Admit to mistakes and share the lessons learned.
- Share the good and the bad of our finances.

Favorite Resource: Read Room & Board's beautiful and brilliant Guiding Principles—http://www.roomandboard.com/room_board/careers/working_at_rnb/guiding_principles.ftl

---

 Favorite Resource: Read Room & Board's beautiful and brilliant Guiding Principles—http://www.roomandboard.com/room_board/careers/working_at_rnb/guiding_principles.ftl

Remember in order to keep your values alive, avoid the biggest values killer: hypocrisy.

You have to be willing to hire *and fire* by your values. Defend and stand by your values even when it's uncomfortable or not the most profitable. It will come back tenfold.

If you find yourself considering an exception, take the time to uncover the unwritten value that uproots the stated value. Should a change be made? For convenience or for ethics?

Plan the Strategic Work, Work the Strategic Plan

 At the top of organizational processes for activating your mission, vision and values is strategic planning. There is a reason for that. Strategic planning is HOW you're going to make your mission and vision a reality while exemplifying your values. It's where the rubber meets the road. When done well it creates momentum by identifying next steps and clarifying why each individual's contribution is important. The strategic plan also nails down the performance expectations of each team member to fulfill the mission and reach the vision.

There are many ways to do strategic planning. My preference is an amalgamation of my own design and of two great resources.

Step 1: Make sure your mission, vision and values are well defined. (See Chapter 3.)

Step 2: Start by giving the questions below to your leadership team. Ask them to ponder the past, present and future prior to meeting. They should garner their teams' input and thoughts on these questions as well.

Step 3: Gather for a half-day and work through these questions. The purpose of this day is to lay out their thinking. Be open to every idea. Don't cull yet.

Evaluate the Past

- What were our accomplishments this last year?
- Did we celebrate them?
- What mistakes did we make this last year?
- Did we evaluate them, learn from them and implement new systems or processes to address them?

Evaluate the Present

- Right now, what's working?
- Can we expand or leverage what's working?
- Right now, what's not working?
- Of these, what is mission critical to address?
- What do we need to do next year about mission critical concerns?
- What are our key actions, activities, products, services, or projects that we need to keep at the forefront?
- Is there anything we need to do differently to make sure these core pieces continue to be nurtured as priorities?

Evaluate Opportunities:

- What projects do we currently have "under construction?"
- How strapped are we right now from a resource perspective (time/energy/money)?
- What's needed to advance our mission and realize our vision?
- Brainstorm strategic opportunities for the organization and for various departments.
- Of these, which three would you prioritize? Why?
- Are any of these as important or more important than current commitments?

Step 4: Let the ideas from the first day ferment for a few days. Then set aside two more half days, one to complete the strategic portion of **The Gazelles One-Page Strategic Plan** and one to complete the implementation portion.*

Favorite Resource: This powerful free tool creates tremendous direction, focus, alignment and accountability for your entire team. You can download this tool and the instructions on this website—www.gazelles.com.

You'll see it's actually two pages. It marries big picture strategy on one page to organizational focus and individual implementation on the other. It funnels from mission, vision and values all the way down to each individual's key performance priorities for the quarter. It makes the master plan succinct and accessible for every employee in the organization. At no point is an employee wondering why they have to accomplish a certain task or goal; they can follow it all the way up the funnel to the mission, vision and values.

*If you've already completed the strategic portion in a prior year, you may not need the full second half-day, as you can simply tweak and adjust this piece each year.

Step 5: Share the strategic plan with the entire team. Speak to the following:

- What were our successes last year? Our struggles? Our learnings?
- What strategies and initiatives were considered for this upcoming year?
- Why were the goals that made the final plan chosen? Why were the other ones not?
- Is there a priority to the goals, or are they all equally important?
- How do the goals support fulfilling our mission?
- How do these goals move us closer to our vision?

Step 6: Align the annual plan with each employee's work. Give each employee a copy of the mostly completed Gazelles One-Page Strategic Plan. Then have each manager meet with each of their team members defining individual work priorities and goals for the quarter. Here employees tangibly learn how their work supports the grand vision.

Make sure the goals you create with employees are action based lead indicators they can control rather than lag results. For example, for the marketing department, you can set a lag goal to increase web traffic. The lead indicator would be the quantity of content posted per week, or the number of industry connections created on LinkedIn, or the number of meaningful booth interactions at a recent conference.

Step 7: Implement a "Cadence of Accountability" from *The Four Disciplines of Execution* by Chris McChesney, Sean Covey and Jim Huling.

 Favorite Resource: *The 4 Disciplines of Execution.* While this book is full of gems, my favorite concept is the "Cadence of Accountability" which can be used in combination with the Gazelles One-Page Strategic Plan.

This process leverages compelling peer pressure and peer support. When done well, this leads to powerful team self-management. It's not all on the manager to check in, encourage or question.

Each week, have a quick stand-up meeting. In that meeting have each individual briefly speak to the one to three strategic bite-size tasks they will accomplish that week towards their quarterly performance priorities. The following week, have each individual speak to their success in accomplishing those tasks (high five!) or not (help needed?) and speak to the tasks they are taking on for the upcoming week. The team witnesses both your success and your struggle.

Step 8: Monthly measure progress, celebrate success and describe the future. At the end of each month take 40 minutes with your team and write down the successes you've accomplished. Then measure how far you all have come towards your team's quarterly goals and annual goals. Consider using the scoreboard concept included in *The 4 Disciplines of Execution.*

Then forward vision what will be accomplished at the end of the upcoming month. "It's October 31st and we have beta tested the new software; we've hired two new developers; we've resolved the bug on the current software; and we won the Halloween contest."

Step 9: Revisit the plan and goals quarterly. When it comes to goals, don't just set it and forget it. Stay focused. Follow up. Adjust.

When made alive and well in the daily workplace experience, mission, vision and values are the deep roots tethering through turmoil and buttressing amid bounty.

Marry Money to the Mission

While integration of the mission, vision and values into processes, systems and strategic planning is key, there is also an important *mindset shift* that needs to happen so your team will buy into your 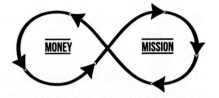 mission as well as your vision. This mindset shift is key as many employees have a negative filter through which they view money in business. Many associate it with greed, power and materialism. It's called cold hard cash, not warm fuzzy funds.

Chances are you talk a lot about money in your organization: the money coming in, the money going out, whether to raise prices, whether to lower them, whether to give raises, whether to hold off, when to make a capital investment, and whether to hire another person. You're constantly looking to protect and expand the financial sustainability and success of your organization.

> "Profit for a company is like oxygen for a person. If you don't have enough of it, you're out of the game. But if you think your life is about breathing, you're really missing something."
>
> **—Peter Drucker,** management consultant, educator and author

However we rarely talk about why money matters. *Here's where you come in.* Connect the money to the mission, the purpose to the profit. Remember, you're not in business to make money. You're in business to fulfill your mission.

Money is energy resulting from successfully fulfilling your mission and the mission is anemic and powerless without money. They depend on and feed one another. As the mission expands, so does the money. As the money expands, so does the mission.

Money is vital water flowing into and through your organization, nurturing growth. It provides for the stability and expansion of your organization and thus the stability and expansion of your mission and purpose. Money creates freedom, ease, comfort, security, and generosity.

Big money equals big impact. Big impact equals big money.

This is the message you want your team to hear. I intentionally use the word "money" instead of "profit." I suggest you do the same with your team. "Money" is visceral. Profit is business speak, a line on a balance sheet.

Show Them the Money—The Invaluable $100 Tool

When I was trying to turn the moving company around, one of the most effective tools I had in my arsenal was what I call my "$100 Tool."

Every year in an all-company meeting I would share our financials with the team using the $100 Tool (described below). It was amazing to see the light bulbs go on. Their entire awareness and attitude would shift. They would come up to me for weeks after this meeting with ideas on how to make and save the company money. They now realized why it was so important to take care of the trucks (cost of truck repairs) and to charge customers for boxes (high margin product) and not to forget moving blankets at the customer's home ($13/each—easily two hours worth of profit.)

Be open with your team about the flow of money. Sharing tells employees they're important. Commitment grows and confusion declines.

Tie decisions to shared financials and your team will more readily support change initiatives—such as when you decide to add a loss leader, reduce the number of products you produce or fire a large client. Without knowledge, employees think the head honcho is lining his basement with gold bricks. They are not aware of the expenses to run an organization. My young movers would think to themselves, "I make $13, and he makes $12, and boss lady's charging $100. Damn! We're the ones out here doing the hard work and she's taking home $75 and ripping us off!" They weren't stupid, they just didn't know what they didn't know.

Some organizations are worried about sharing their financials, either because they're struggling or very successful. Sharing financials when you're in trouble is the only way to engage your employees' support. It helps them understand the urgency in your voice. Your employees aren't stupid. They know if something's off. Sharing the financials puts fears to rest because they can see what you see and participate in generating money making and saving solutions.

If you're on the flip side and very successful and fear employees will want a bigger piece of the pie, communicate your growth plan and the need for cash to fund investments in equipment, technology, personnel or assets. Frame that extra money as a shared savings account. If you're not looking to grow, make sure your people are well compensated and appreciated. This may also be a good time to share the risks and rewards of owning a business.

 Action Jackson: Use the **$100 Tool** to Share Your Financials in a Tangible, Accurate Way

1. Get 100 one dollar bills.

2. On a flip chart or white board, break down by percentage your high-level income streams:

   o $43—local moves

   o $37—national moves

   o $12—storage

   o $5—boxes

   o $3—insurance

3. Break down by percentage your **high-level expenses** (fuel, truck repairs, truck maintenance, furniture repairs, regulatory fees, marketing and networking, utilities, insurance, rent, payroll—include in payroll workers compensation, payroll taxes and benefits.)

4. **Speak about how your organization makes money.** Share which verticals, products and services are the most and least profitable. Explain why you choose to keep those that are less profitable—loss leader, bread and butter, competitive edge.

5. **Then talk through expenses.** As you detail each expense, hand out the dollar bills to individual employees. Saying for example:

   o You are my landlord you receive $4 for rent.

   o You are my accountant you receive $2.

   o You are my utilities you receive $5.

6. **Speak to employee payroll, payroll taxes, work comp and benefits last.** Employees are always wowed by the comparatively large piece of the pie that is directly theirs.

7. **Then show them, with the dollars left in your hand, how much profit is left.** Explain how this profit is taxed, leaving a net profit and how that money has to be used to pay off debt as well as to reinvest

in the company to spur growth. Explain how it is *this* money—the money that's left over—that funds raises, better benefits, new uniforms, additional staff, or new equipment.

8. **Help them understand which numbers they can impact and which ones they can't.** You want them to leave knowing how they individually can help the organization make and save money.

9. Depending on your team, it can also be valuable to **explain the difference between profit and cash flow.** You may want to share the role of revenue to profit. Clarify that without profit, revenue is wheel spinning. Small increases in revenue beyond goal can cause exponential increases in profit due to the relatively static nature of overhead costs.

Owners tend to wonder how to represent their compensation when sharing financials. In the process above, simply roll your compensation into payroll.

....

 Favorite Resource: If you want to take this experience to the next level, consider not just sharing the financials, but implementing Open Book Management as described in Jack Stack's book *The Great Game of Business*.

Embrace money as mission nourishing energy and talk about money openly.

Activating your mission, vision and values fills the tank and fires up your workplace engine. It means when the rubber hits the road, your team is ready for the long, horizon-expanding adventure.

Chapter 5

Strengthen Shared Identity and Interdependency

- Instill Tribe Trifecta—Organization, Team, Individual

- Bolster Known, Matter and Included

- Illuminate Interdependency Awareness

- Discuss, Illustrate and Ground Interdependency Awareness

- Stand on Common Ground

- Launch an Ice Bucket Challenge

- Choose Your Tattoo

- Cultivate Crew, Not Passengers

- Reframe the Family Fallacy

- Practice Meaningful Appreciation and Recognition

- Try on Peer-to-Peer Recognition

| Supervisor | Co-workers | Meaning/ Job Fit | Impact | Organizational Fit |

"When we try to pick out anything by itself, we find it hitched to everything else in the Universe."

—John Muir, naturalist and philosopher

You've been there. The puzzle missing a piece is incomplete. The piece missing a puzzle is useless. Now imagine your organization's mission is the puzzle, and your team is the pieces. Your organization is a conscious community brought together to fulfill a shared purpose. This purpose cannot be accomplished alone. It is core to your team's shared identity. This chapter outlines the role of the individual within the organization and of the organization within the individual.

Instill Tribe Trifecta—Organization, Team, Individual

Many workplace culture issues stem from dissonance between what's best for the individual, what's best for the team and what's best for the organization. When aligned, you've got cultural magic.

The key: loyalty and commitment to what's best for the organization must supersede team and individual agendas. Teams need to yield to the organization while individuals need to yield to the team.

HOWEVER this only works when what's best for the organization is also what's best for the team and the individual. It is a virtuous circle.

In order for individuals to yield personal interest, the organization must consistently demonstrate it has the best interest of its team members in mind. Organizational consideration can show up in many ways, as disparate as training, an unexpected bonus, firing toxic employees, real cream for coffee, and soft toilet paper in the bathroom.

For example, under his leadership, Doug Conant, the CEO of Campbell Soup, transformed a toxic corporate culture and a sagging stock price into a Wall Street favorite that also scored high on employee engagement. "You can only win in the marketplace if you win in the workplace first," he noted. How did he do that?

"We made a major commitment to training and development, which was part of a philosophy we called "The Campbell Promise." If you're asking people to do extraordinary things, they have to see you leaning in to help them learn and grow," he explained to an interviewer. "Otherwise, your message will fall on deaf ears over time. We had high expectations of people, and we couldn't expect them to value the company's agenda if we didn't tangibly demonstrate that we valued their agenda as well."

When teams band together for the greater good, they bond. They bond over their shared experience, commitment and loyalty. In moments of struggle, they take pride in their moral courage. For instance, I have heard employees say they would rather be part of a team that took a 10 percent pay cut rather than suffer survivor's guilt of laid off co-workers.

One of the most destructive decisions a company can make is providing *unwarranted* preferential treatment to a single employee or department. When an organization puts an individual first, it undermines the foundational bond of "we're all in this together." This results in morale mutiny. Just think about the last time a highly skilled toxic employee received a raise in hopes they would turn their attitude around.

Next time you're stuck focusing on an individual employee challenge, ask the following:

- What's best for the success of the organization?
- For the team?
- For the individual?
- Can we simultaneously accomplish all three *without* tying ourselves in knots?
- If not, what are the facts of the misalignment?

Bolster Known, Matter and Included

Never forget your organization is a group of individuals. Individuals with their own assumptions, backgrounds, beliefs, desires, experiences, needs, values, priorities, perspectives, and preferences. And yet, most everyone has a core desire to be known, to matter and to be included.

For most Americans, this core desire is not being fulfilled. The National Science Foundation reported in its "General Social Survey" that more than half of Americans have no one outside their immediate family with whom they can discuss important matters and share confidences and triumphs. Social isolation leads to depression and disease, while emotional intimacy leads to joy and health.

Your workplace has the opportunity to be a place where your people connect beyond superficial interactions. A place where they are known, where they matter and where they feel included.

Being known means you're not invisible, easily ignored or forgotten. You're thought of, remembered, considered. Your team knows who you are. They know your goofy quirks, your dog's name and your obsession with strawberries. They know what they can count on you for and they know where you struggle. You're missed when you're not there.

Knowing you matter gives life purpose. It also has ramifications. If you go the extra mile, it matters. If you slack, it matters. When your effort is appreciated, when your results are noticed, when your mistakes impact your team, you know you play a significant role in the success of your organization. Your team witnesses you, sometimes rubbernecking and covering one eye, sometimes providing testimony. This directly feeds the critical factor of Impact.

Feeling included creates a sense of belonging. Your presence is desired. You are not alone. You're part of a tribe. You know the fight song, you know the unwritten rules as well as the inside jokes. You're part of a team that exponentially expands your individual contribution, making you greater than yourself.

At the core of this reciprocal, symbiotic beauty of an extraordinary workplace culture is this individual need to be known, to matter and to be included. When those needs are met, the foundation is laid to fulfill the organization's needs. One feeds the other. They are interdependent.

Illuminate Interdependency Awareness

We're all in this together, right?

Interdependency awareness means every individual understands both how their role feeds the success of the whole and how the whole nurtures their success.

Think about the childhood game Mouse Trap. Piece by piece children build a complicated system to trap a mouse. The sexiest piece in the game is the silver ball. It pops out of the bucket, rolls down the stairs and through the curvy slide causing the rest of the parts to play their role and ultimately trap the mouse. Yet the silver ball is completely inconsequential without the rest of the system. (Similar to the rock star performer in your organization.)

> *Each piece is mission critical to the success of the whole and the whole is mission critical to each piece.*

Each person on your team needs to understand the importance of their position in fulfilling the mission.

Why does the organization need George, the administrative assistant? How does his role contribute to our success? "Without George we wouldn't be sane. He keeps us all organized and on task. Without George it would take us months instead of weeks to accomplish a project."

If you ever find yourself unable to answer this question—as brutal as it sounds—you have uncovered an unnecessary expense.

If you have departments that don't get along, it's often because one views their role as more important than the other. In the moving industry, it is common to have the frontline crew and the office staff squabble. Movers perceive the office staff as lazily sitting at a comfy air-conditioned desk, while the office staff perceives the crew as replaceable unskilled labor. Lack of consideration and finger pointing is common.

To avoid this destructive tension, I created respect and appreciation between the two by stressing how challenging and important each job was. The crew understood the constant logistical crisis the office managed when a client changed dates or a truck failed to start. The office understood the perseverance and problem solving required to take a piano up a switch back staircase in the dead heat of summer.

"We're all on the same team, wearing the same jersey," I reminded them. They had to count on one another to fulfill our mission and brand promise to provide "Peace of Mind, All in One Piece." When a problem would arise, rather than throw one another under the bus, they would seek one another's support.

Individuals do not work in a vacuum, nor do teams. To have an employee think, "I'm all good" because they have reached individual performance goals is narrow-minded and shortsighted. This is part of why departments sink into silos and become territorial about their resources. They feel they can "protect" themselves from the rest of the organization's performance. Or in worst case scenarios, they think they can prove their value in comparison to other teams, becoming competitive and even at times undermining one another's efforts.

Everyone is in the same boat. Poking holes is suicide.

Action Jackson: Discuss, Illustrate and Ground
Interdependency Awareness

First have your team watch the three-minute OK GO music video of
the song "This Too Shall Pass" on YouTube—make sure it's the Rube
Goldberg version—and discuss the factors that made this teamwork
successful. Cover these insights:

- Each piece is mission-critical to the whole. No one piece can say, "I
  don't feel like showing up today."

- The whole is mission critical to each piece. Each piece is
  inconsequential without the rest of the system.

- Each piece is impacted by the piece before it and impacts the piece
  after it.

- A clear vision of the shared purpose.

- The importance of collaboration, communication and coordination.

- The importance of commitment, perseverance and grit.

- Rhythm and cadence shifts as needed.

- There's easy forgiveness and learning from mistakes—paint on the
  band and multiple broken TVs.

- Lots of planning, trying on and tweaking—commitment to
  continuous improvement along with a sense of humor.

- The importance of the "back of house" to the "front of the house."
  While four people are in the spotlight, it took the entire crew to
  make it successful.

Then talk through your organization's cycle of work. Have each
department speak to their role and their challenges. Which departments clash? Sales and operations? Engineering and manufacturing?
What beliefs underlie the struggle?

Have each department kindly and candidly make three requests
regarding what they need from other departments to be more
successful.

Stand on Common Ground

Some organizations feel they can't build a cohesive culture because their employees are diverse. I've heard: "It's hard because they're all so different. We have employees who work in the office and those who are out in the field. Our employees come from different educational, social, economic, age and race backgrounds. They have different priorities and preferences."

At the heart of divisiveness is separateness, me vs. you, us vs. them. Whenever disunity begins to take hold of your team, lean on common ground. Everybody wants to:

- Support themselves and/or their families.
- Contribute.
- Be part of something that's meaningful and bigger than themselves.
- Do work that makes them proud.
- Work for an organization that makes them proud.
- Be acknowledged and appreciated for a job well done.
- Be better tomorrow than they are today.
- Have someone who will champion their potential and who believes in them.
- Work well with and enjoy their co-workers.

Your employees have chosen to work here. Remind them. We're all on the same team, wearing the same jersey. We're all doing the best we can do.

Launch an Ice Bucket Challenge

There's a reason the ice bucket challenge was so successful. Think about it. Everyone who played experienced the following:

- Making a difference by plugging into a cause bigger than yourself.

- Being part of a tribe with a similar commitment.

- Being chosen to participate and choosing others.

- Sharing your pride that you're a part of the tribe.

- Being witnessed by that tribe through video.

- Having fun, shared joy in the battle against the disease.

Now think about your team.

What kind of ice bucket challenge could you create for your team?

I knew someone of a team who needed open-heart surgery.

His company bought everyone Fitbits. For every one million steps taken in the month, the company donated $1,000 to his surgery. In the five months leading up to the surgery, the team took five million steps and together raised $5,000 for their co-worker.

There are at least seven wins here:

1. The financial support the employee received.

2. The sense of contributing to something bigger than yourself (my steps alone are not enough).

3. The sense of camaraderie and team interdependency—we're in this together.

4. The warm fuzzy felt through participating.

5. The health and well being created by all those steps.

6. The sense of winning, and being on a winning and caring team.

7. The cost of the Fitbits and the donation were easily covered by the increase in productivity due to improved wellness and morale.

Choose Your Tattoo

What would a tattoo of your organization's logo say about the person sporting it? About their personality, reputation and identity?

Consider, your employees are in essence tattooed with your logo. They assume, contribute to and represent this identity in their personal and professional lives. Now consider, how do they assume and represent this identity? With gusto and pride, detached nonchalance or skittish shame and awkward unease?

Organizational culture fit is the alignment of one's self-identity with the organization's identity.

Consider Harley-Davidson. What would a Harley-Davidson tattoo say about the person displaying it? Cool, rugged individualism, promise for the open road, (safe) rebellion. Consider a few of Harley Davidson's taglines:

- "Ride among us"
- "Proud of our heritage and individuality"
- "One big happy (very cool) family"

Many people get the Harley-Davidson logo as a tattoo. Why? It's a powerful combination of individualism and tribe (us, our heritage, family). This branding extends throughout the company. Each Harley-Davidson dealership has its own shop logo that is both a recognizable brand and an individual statement. Their identity provides the best of both worlds: self-actualization within a community.

When Choosing Your Tattoo...

1. **Know your identity.** If you struggled to answer the tattoo question, look to your mission, vision and values.

2. **Be intentional in encouraging both individualism as well as belonging to the group.**

3. **Leverage human nature.** As social creatures, we participate in communities because we want:

   o To be part of something bigger than ourselves

   o Fellowship

   o Validation of our choices

   o Our individual contribution to be magnified

   o Recognition, meaning or status

   How does your organization fulfill these basic desires?

4. **Carefully consider your group context**—examine your (spoken and unspoken) agreements, commitments, guiding principles and rules of engagement.

   o What's allowed and not allowed?

   o Who gets to be a member? Who doesn't?

   o What do you stand for? Stand against?

   o What are your principles for working together?

   o What's your common language, team colors, secret handshake, or fight song?

5. **Don't force it. When it's a fit, it's a fit.** Notice Harley-Davidson does not require compliance, conformity, nor dependency. When it's a good culture fit you don't have to manipulate or mandate your employees to participate.

Cultivate Crew Not Passengers

Take a moment and imagine your team in a rowboat. Is your entire team rowing with fervor, in rhythm and in the right direction? Perhaps even singing the company fight song in unison?

Or are some:

- Simply passengers along for the ride (perhaps dead weight)?

- Rowing really hard—but in the wrong direction?

- Tempted to throw down an anchor in frustration?

- Engaged in a paddle battle, hitting one another with their oars?

- Trying to push others overboard?

- New and simply trying to learn the rhythm?

- Looking to jump ship?

Reframe the Family Fallacy

When organizations pride themselves on being "like a family," they often have familial dysfunctions. There's usually codependency, enabled bad behavior, a sense of sibling rivalry and a lack of accountability.

The reality is your employees are not your family. (In those cases where they are, that's a whole 'nother book.) There's no promise to love or employ your employees unconditionally. You pay for performance. People are not entitled to employment and you are not entitled to their work.

You are not responsible for, nor guilty of, the choices your employees make in their personal lives. You are not responsible for their life circumstances. You can feel and express empathy, compassion and kindness when times are tough. At the end of the day there is an employment agreement that binds your relationship, not blood.

Yet most of us value real-deal, authentic connection with those in our daily sphere. When we say we're like a family, we're saying we want the positive experience of family. We want family spirit. This slight distinction is key. Instead of saying, "we're a family" or "we're like a family," try on "we have family spirit."

I appreciate Zappos core value definition of "Positive Team and Family Spirit:" *We watch out for each other, care for each other, and go above and beyond for each other because we believe in each other and we trust each other.*

On the flip side, some companies avoid family spirit and emotional intimacy fearing they won't be objective when making hard decisions about non-performing employees. There is anxiety that already difficult conversations will become even more difficult if close relationships make the exchange more personal. However the alternative is bleak—cold, distant, sanitized, "safe from feelings," work relationships. With family spirit, it will be messy and uncomfortable at times, yet you'll have real relationships where warm loyalty, camaraderie and fellowship can grow.

Practice Meaningful Appreciation and Recognition

You're the shizzle! No, really you are. You're almost through Chapter 5. Most people never actually read the books they purchase. Many have the best of intentions, but you see things through! Your commitment and dedication to your team and their workplace experience makes my work meaningful. Thank you.

Appreciation is noticing, acknowledging and giving testimony when your employees go above and beyond. This is the upside of accountability. Appreciation affirms that an individual's contribution matters. You witness their effort and value their contribution.

Where are you on the appreciation spectrum? For some managers, appreciation is so rare teams wonder if anyone notices their work. On the other end, managers who say "thank you" too often can appear inauthentic.

Perhaps you don't need or expect kudos for doing your job. You figure you get paid and that's sufficient. If this is you, you are rare. Most people want their efforts to be witnessed and appreciated, especially when they go above and beyond. Not because they *need* it, but because it feels good. It's a warm fuzzy. Here's the deal: there's no reason not to appreciate and celebrate an employee's achievement. It shows you care. For free. It feeds the desire to be known and to feel one's work and effort provides value.

I receive a lot of questions about appreciation. Here's a few of the most common ones and my answers:

When do I appreciate an employee? Should I say thank you for the obvious? For example, "Thanks for coming in on time," to someone who is usually late?

No. Don't praise average work. Don't praise to motivate someone. It comes off as condescending. Instead, say "thank you" to an employee or a team when they:

- Exceed expectations.
- Take on a challenge or learn a new skill.
- Complete milestones on a difficult project.
- Take the initiative to improve a process or resolve a problem.

Lastly, share the love when a customer, co-worker or vendor calls out someone. Be timely in your appreciation.

If I thank one person, do I need to thank the one sitting next to them too?

Yes. So don't praise in public. Praise one-on-one. When you praise in a group, there's a good chance others have made efforts deserving of your praise, but you don't know about it. Don't risk making others feel invisible or left out, undermining their sense of belonging to the team. (One exception to this rule is next.)

When is it appropriate to publicly praise someone?

Publicly praise when you're looking to shift a habit on your team or to encourage candor. (More at the end of this chapter.) Also praise work anniversaries. Highlight anniversary celebrations more than birthday celebrations since they are unique to work, earned and demonstrate loyalty. Praise that person's contributions over the past year. You can also publicly pass on the praise from a customer, vendor or co-worker at a team meeting.

Do I need to write a thank-you note?

No. Too often, they're on a to-do-list that never gets done. Instead, put this book down and walk over to (or call) your stellar employee and tell them how much you appreciate their work and why. Verbal communication enables meaningful pauses and intonation that can't be captured in a thank you note or email. With that said, I also swear by the power of a Post-it Note. (They even have sparkly ones.) A Post-it Note is less daunting and likely to stick around your employee's work area for weeks to come. A thank you note often ends up in a drawer. I also love high-fives.

What should I say besides "thank you" or "you rock!"?

Say what it meant to you and to the success of larger goals. Express the immediate and long-term impact of their contribution.

Here are some examples: Thank you so much...

- For handling that issue yesterday. Your efforts helped me to focus and finish a critical report for the board that's been hanging over my head.
- Because you went above and beyond to meet the finish line early, our client was thrilled and referred us, which means we'll meet our sales goals for the month.
- Your leadership and integrity in this situation means we won't lose such a key account. You saved our bacon.

- Without your willingness to stay late, there's no way we could have finished this project on time for our customer. Guaranteed we would have gotten an ear full.

Does there need to be some sort of reward to go with it too? Shouldn't I put my money where my mouth is?

No. Witnessing and acknowledgment are the keys, not reciprocity. Neither a company jacket nor a gift card can honor staying late three weeks in a row. Your good intentions will backfire. There is pride in being the type of person who will go the extra mile. Expand this intrinsic warm fuzzy with your words and your emotions.

Now if you just can't help yourself and you know this person would love a gift card from Joe's Cafe or Golf Gopher, then go ahead. BUT, don't have it slow down your response time and do mention it's a "token" of your appreciation. Don't create the expectation of reciprocity—the idea that every extra effort earns a reward. This leads to entitlement. Let it be a lovely small surprise. Don't have that surprise be branded merchandise. It's not personal. Also if the tchotchke is coveted, others will feel left out. Instead, *gift* logoed items to your entire team.

Don't do what I did. The December of the recession, money was brutally tight at the moving company. No one was buying or selling houses meaning no one was moving. My guys weren't getting many hours and were feeling the pinch at just the wrong time. A couple of years prior we gave warm, name-embroidered jackets. The year before, we gave each employee $100. Although we were really tight, I felt like

More Appreciation Ideas

- Talk up. Share the employee's efforts with leadership or someone in another department. Request that they tell the stellar employee he's the one everyone owes a big thank you to for finally figuring out how to get the product shipped before noon. The element of surprise goes a long way.
- Connect them with a mentor who can help them advance in their career.

- Offer them an opportunity to learn more via an outside conference, course or workshop.

- Give them an extra long lunch break or a Friday afternoon off.

- Ask them to attend an interesting event in your stead.

- Write them a letter of praise recognizing specific contributions and accomplishments and send a copy to senior management and put it in their personnel file.

- When someone has spent long hours at work, send a letter of thanks to her family. Consider picking up the pizza tab.

- Arrange for an outstanding employee to have lunch with the head honcho.

- Inscribe a favorite book as a gift.

- Give them a membership or subscription to a magazine or journal that relates to their work.

- Find out what they want to learn, accomplish or create that would benefit the team. Be clear on budget availability. Then have them research learning opportunities and ask them to brief you on their findings.

I had to do something. At most, I could afford $25 per team member. That felt like too little to give in cash. I tried to think of something they would all like. One of guys' dad sold specialty beef jerky, magically $25 for a box.

The leadership team cooked everyone and their families a hearty holiday meal. I stood up and thanked everyone for their hard work and continued effort in the face of tough times. Then I handed out the beef jerky. They responded as if I'd spit in their face. It was horrible.

I should have mitigated expectations. I should have been straight with our team. I should have given nothing—nothing but my heartfelt appreciation and acknowledgement of their personal hardship. Nobody wanted jerky. They wanted more work, the same thing I wanted for them and for our company. Needless to say, I ate crow jerky for years to come.

If I thank them, won't they ask for a raise?

Maybe. Whether it's a serious request or said jokingly, set up a time for a compensation conversation.

Should we do "Employee of the Month?"

No. It acknowledges only one person, leaving others feeling left out. What happens if, in all honesty, the same person earns the honor month after month? Or there's five people to recognize, or no one? Overall, formalized employee recognition programs are rarely effective. They feel forced. I've also seen programs in which everyone is acknowledged, making it feel weird like, "everyone gets a trophy!"

Try Peer-to-Peer Recognition— REI Anderson Award

I've often said formal employee recognition programs don't work. I repeated this statement at an HR conference where I was presenting and asked if anyone had a formal employee recognition program that did work. One hand went up out of 300.

This hand belonged to a store manager at REI and she shared their process for a formal employee recognition program that is honoring, meaningful and inspiring.

This annual employee recognition program is called the Anderson Award. It's named after the Founders of REI, Lloyd and Mary Anderson.

Four key aspects make this award successful:

1. It is a peer-to-peer award. Employees nominate other employees.

2. Employees nominate those they believe live REI's core values and co-op spirit.

3. Everyone, except for managers, directors and VPs, is eligible.

4. About one in 100 employees receives this award so it's truly a special honor.

How the process works:

- Anyone can submit a nomination.

- The store manager chooses a peer committee to evaluate the nominations and select a recipient. Managers do *not* sit on this committee. The committee chair is often last year's recipient. This committee not only makes the final selection, they also decide how they will announce each nominee at the holiday store meeting, making it special each year.

- The store recipient is then flown to REI Headquarters for three days to interact with other recipients. There a stone, engraved with their name, is added to the walkway at headquarters. They become a permanent part of the company's history.

One more idea—at the moving company we created bright yellow business cards with the word "You're a Rock Star." Any time a crew member delighted a customer, they would receive a Rock Star card with a vivid description on the back. Office staff would receive cards for resolving challenging logistics and calming frustrated clients. Everyone received them when they went above and beyond the call of duty—covering an unexpected shift, staying late, keeping a good attitude in freezing weather. Anyone could bestow a card upon anyone. Then once a quarter, everyone except leadership could submit their cards for a drawing for a variety of prizes—baseball tickets, a paid day off, dinner for the family.

You do not share blood with your team. What you do share is all of your circumstances, experiences and choices that brought you to this place, to this time, to this team and they to you. Your team is a conscious community that's been brought together to fulfill on a shared purpose. Interdependency deepens the appreciation for the effort each individual brings to the table. It's an awesome potluck, one that would be incomplete without Mary's famous cheese dip.

Chapter 6

Shift Accountability

- The Ability to Count

- Adopt the Workable Integrity Checklist

- Sip Truth Serum

- Clarify Character and Competency Expectations

- Renounce Unkind Niceness

- Be a Stand for Someone's Success

- Explain *How* to Change

- Manage an OverDescriber

- Know When to Stop Investing in an Employee

- Fire Toxic Rainmakers

- Be Intolerant to Improve Your Culture

- Stop Workplace Bullying

Supervisor   **Co-workers**   **Impact**   **Organizational Support**   **Organizational Fit**

> *"It may be hard for an egg to turn into a bird: it would be a jolly sight harder for it to learn to fly while remaining an egg. We are like eggs at present. And you cannot go on indefinitely being just an ordinary, decent egg. We must be hatched or go bad."*

> **—C.S. Lewis,** novelist and poet

The Ability to Count

Accountability is a tough term. What do you think of when you hear the word? I've heard: belittling, finger wagging, someone watching your every move, feeling of being in trouble or having done something wrong. Who's to blame? They must be held accountable! Even Thesaurus.com's first synonym for hold accountable is "place blame for wrongdoing."

Not exactly positive, happy dance material. But accountability is key to an extraordinary workplace culture. Holding people accountable is to witness both when someone is being successful and when they are struggling. When you see success, follow up with meaningful appreciation and recognition as outlined in the last chapter. High performers, and those who are set up for success, love accountability.

However, if you have someone on your team who is struggling, you've likely been asked to "hold them accountable." But what does that even mean? Hold them in check? Hold one's feet to the fire? Consider instead, holding their hand. Support, coach and guide them to success. To a point. (You knew that was coming, didn't you?)

If someone isn't pulling their weight or isn't being kind and there's no reaction, things get wonky fast. When you say nothing, you give unsaid permission to perpetuate bad behaviors. Subpar behavior or performance becomes normal, accepted. A new, low standard is set. Identity is questioned and pride is lost. Mediocrity sets in. Caring slips.

Let's be clear who's accountable for accountability—you are. Everyone on your team is responsible for being a stand for the team's success. However, the leader sets the bar. If you don't define expectations, no one else will. You are the catalyst. When you go there, they will follow.

Shift your team's thinking about accountability. Create a new definition. Make it the "ability to count," the ability to have someone's effort and energy count, to make a difference and an impact. Make it clear you will not let circumstances define commitment. Regardless of the weather, the economy, being short staffed, etc.—every day they choose how they're going to show up and prioritize next steps towards the finish line.

Adopt the Workable Integrity Checklist

A lack of integrity is often judged unforgiveable:

- He's a hypocrite.

- She's a liar.

- He can't be counted on.

- You can't trust her; she says one thing and does another.

These character judgments are part of the reason so few people admit to mistakes and lean on weak excuses for lack of follow through. This fear of being judged quietly destroys workplace cultures.

Yet we're all human. We've all failed to keep a New Year's resolution. We've all arrived late to an appointment. We've all had the best of intentions turn sideways. Our nature is to forgive someone who comes to us with hat in hand, owns their rubbish and commits to a different future way of being.

Imagine approaching integrity as a question of workability, mission critical to performance, rather than as a question of morality, ethics or character. This profound distinction comes from, "Integrity: a Positive Model that Incorporates the Normative Phenomena of Morality, Ethics, and Legality," by Werner H. Erhard, Michael C. Jensen, and Steve Zaffron (unpublished paper at http://ssrn.com/abstract=920265; copyright 2005–2009 Werner Erhard, Michael C. Jensen, Steve Zaffron).

Another way to think about accountability is to call it workable integrity. Accountability is about being count-on-able. When people follow through and do what they say they are going to do, work is easier.

Next time you're struggling with someone on your team, pull out the Workable Integrity Checklist inspired by the work of Werner Erhard (see the above article on integrity). Walk through each item. Where is the main disconnect? Then help them figure out how to repair it.

The Workable Integrity Checklist

☐ Nothing hidden.

☐ Being truthful and honest.

☐ Working from an empowering context.*

☐ Doing well what you do.

☐ Doing the work as it was meant to be done or better without cutting corners.

☐ Honoring your word.

☐ Doing what you know to do.

☐ Doing what you said on time.

☐ Doing what others expect you to do even if you haven't said you would do it.**

☐ Speaking up immediately when you realize you won't be doing this as expected or won't be doing it at all.

*Empowering context refers to doing the work agreeably. You're not disparaging, undermining or bemoaning the task. For example, a non-empowering context would be:

- "I'm only doing this because he said I had to do it."

- "This is stupid, but I'll do it anyway."

- "I think this is a waste of time, but someone's got to do it."

An empowering context means actively choosing and taking on a task, enjoyable or not, because you know the value and impact it brings to the work at hand. We are all responsible for our words and actions. If you think a task is a waste of time, come from a place of curiosity. Ask questions. Ask why the task is worthwhile. Explain to team members why a task is important.

**This is the one where people bristle. What? I didn't agree to this. Why do I have to do it? Simple. It's what's expected of you. If you are aware of those expectations, and unless you negotiate changes, you are responsible for meeting them. Think about the company bowling party when one of your key people didn't show up. Your expectation was he would participate or communicate if he wasn't attending. It's the same logic parents hear from children: "You just said I have to go to bed, you didn't say I have to go to sleep."

Sip Truth Serum

The last box to check on the Workability Integrity Checklist is best represented by a conversation I had with a client who runs a large construction company. A marketing initiative started in the slow season was not just being put on the backburner, but let go, during high production. Some might find this short sighted from a strategy standpoint. Others might see it as a lack of integrity.

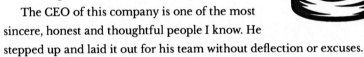

The CEO of this company is one of the most sincere, honest and thoughtful people I know. He stepped up and laid it out for his team without deflection or excuses.

"If we're really honest, the truth is we're not going to follow through on this marketing effort," he said. "When we were slow, I said this was a priority and it was. Now it's not, and it's simply not going to happen. That's really the truth here. And to say we're going to pick the ball back up and run with it would be to delay the truth and create false hope. I want to acknowledge all of you who have put a lot of effort towards this work. I apologize for work wasted. Priorities have shifted and we need to shift with them. Lastly, know I'm aware we still need a long-term strategy to secure steady work."

Naming this truth was powerful permission for the team. The monkey was off their back. They could stop feeling guilty for not making progress on a project that didn't require further attention. It focused them on what mattered going forward.

What's worse than walking away is renegotiating over and over and then never completing the task. Ever experience the self-defeating daily recommitment to a habit until you finally don't even believe yourself? Many employees can name a promise or commitment the organization has been making for years and never fulfilled. The intentions are good. But the continuous lack of integrity chips away at an organization's credibility. Clay feet become quicksand. Have the humility to pivot when needed. Be less committed to "looking good." Do what's best. Speak the truth and eat some short-term crow.

Clarify Character and Competency Expectations

Excellent leadership and seasoned managers share a common belief: **the belief in human potential.**

They believe in their people and they set the bar higher than individuals would for themselves. High expectations lead to high performance. When you give someone a difficult task, they take it as an assessment of their ability. They then increase their level of effort to prove you right.

Employees want to be successful. Expectations allow your team to self-assess their performance and feel a sense of accomplishment, pride and motivation to do more, better, faster. When expectations are unclear, nobody knows where they stand. The unknown leads to rumors, paranoia and mistakes. Clarify your character and competency expectations. What does it take to be a member of your team?

On the character side:

- What attitudes and behaviors are expected?
- What values and principles for working together need to be practiced?

On the competency side:

- What skills and expertise are needed to be successful in each position?
- What does excellence look like? What does subpar performance look like?

When you think of your team, how does each person fare on the character side? On the competency side? Your best players are excellent at both. Then you have those whose competency is extraordinary, but whose character is lacking. They can be jerks and at times toxic. Be a stand for their success, show them their blind spot and then coach them through it. Share how to shift their character (more on page 69).

Then you have the opposite, those the team thoroughly enjoys but whose capability is subpar. Get them additional training or a skills mentor to support the critical factor of Meaning/Job Fit. It's impossible to feel like your work is meaningful and worthwhile if you can't successfully complete it.

At the end of the day, though, everyone on your team needs character and competence. If the character doesn't shift and if the competency doesn't improve, they are not a good fit.

This can be heartbreaking, especially if you like the individual but their work simply isn't good enough. However, put yourself in their shoes. They want to do a good job. They care about the work and the team, and yet, the position just doesn't leverage their strengths. Repeated failure is painful and demolishes self-esteem. To keep them on the team is being cruel to be kind.

At the moving company, I made the common mistake of promoting an awesome producer to a management position. Before his promotion, he took tremendous pride in his acumen. His work was admired and he was the "go-to" guy for all things related to national moves. After his promotion, he struggled. Mistakes were made. The team questioned his ability to do the job.

He went from rock star to rock bottom in a matter of weeks. Luckily, he was relieved when I demoted him with dignity to his previous position. The Peter Principle applies here. What makes a stunning technician does not make a stunning manager of technicians.

If you have someone on your team right now who has neither character nor competency, time to do everyone a favor and set them free.

Renounce Unkind Niceness

Directly communicating concerns to someone requires vulnerability. Vulnerability is scary. So instead, people avoid, couch, lie, placate, agree and then turn and tell someone else what they really think, seeking validation for their feelings.

Most of us would agree we would rather have someone speak with us directly about concerns than tear down our character behind our back and, yet, the latter happens more often than the former.

The fear of being disliked is the root of backstabbing and why peer accountability within an organization is rare. When I meet with low-performing teams I ask the following:

- Have you failed to hold a co-worker accountable to be "nice" because you didn't want to hurt their feelings?

- Did you go ahead and do the work yourself, making assumptions about why the other person didn't complete it?

- Did you then feel resentful?

- Did you make comments about that person's inability to do their work to your spouse, co-workers, or supervisor?

If you did, consider *your co-worker never had the chance to respond or correct their behavior because you never spoke to them directly.*

We often think people won't like us if we hold them accountable, and yet we all have a story of someone who was brave enough to bring a blind spot to our attention, an act that changed how we acted and who we were. These changes often lead to self-actualization and richer relationships.

Chef Francis Mallmann remembers how the president of Cartier, the jewelry company, took him aside after a meal. The executive privately told him he didn't enjoy the food. Mallmann was trying to be a French chef, but the food was not French.

In that moment, Mallmann saw his blind spot.

He changed his path, cooking with fire, a nod to his Argentinian roots. "He had read in my life something that I didn't know but that was very important," Mallmann recalls. "Nowadays I feel that one of my responsibilities is to tell young chefs those sort of messages, not in a harsh way. But we must because you don't forget those things. They help you grow in life."

When I was running the moving company, I struggled with one of my right-hand employees. He was extraordinary, until he wasn't. He was struggling through a divorce made even more horrible by a custody battle. In an effort to be empathetic and understanding, I gave him space. Space to take care of paperwork, lawyers and court appointments. The team was also empathetic, but became overwhelmed with issues resulting from his lack of performance. I not only permitted his behavior, I enabled it. I regularly defended him to other team members. He was losing credibility with the team and I was losing credibility as a leader because I wasn't holding him accountable.

I finally walked into his office, sat down and said, "Listen, I know you're going through this awful divorce, but we need you. We count on you to lead operations. If you don't step it up we can't be successful. In an effort to support you these last few months, I've let the team down by not bringing this to your attention sooner. I'm struggling with how to support you and also meet the needs of our team. I'd like to sit down before the end of the week and figure out how to get you the support you need while still accomplishing the work we need you to do. If you need to opt out, if you simply don't have the mental capacity to lead operations right now, I understand."

I was shocked. Instead of feeling like I was kicking him while he was down, his demeanor changed. He sat up straighter. His eyes brightened.

All of a sudden he understood that he was both needed and wanted, and that his contribution mattered. His self-esteem had been suffering. He simply needed to know he was an important part of our team. In an effort to be kind, I had done him a disservice. The next day he came in ready to be the confident and capable colleague we always knew him to be.

Be a Stand for Someone's Success

Holding someone accountable tells them you value their contribution, that their work makes a difference.

If they don't do their work, or don't do it well, it matters. They matter.

When you're truly committed to someone else's success, you hold them accountable. You help them be the best they can be by communicating when something is amiss. To not say anything is to sit quietly by and watch as an individual's work credibility deteriorates.

I've seen an employee get fired because he smelled. To this day he still doesn't know the real reason why he was let go nor the reason why his co-workers avoided him at lunchtime. People were too kind to suggest he use mouthwash and deodorant. He would have kept his job if one person had simply said, "Dude, you might want to consider different deodorant. I'm just telling you because I would want someone to tell me."

When done with the intent to support someone in their success, reaching out to a fellow team member and making them aware of a blind spot is a kindness. You hope someone will tell you if you have spinach in your teeth. Or that you smell or you're overly chatty or you're not meeting performance expectations. While traditionally this is officially the manager's responsibility, in extraordinary workplace cultures everyone is a stand for everyone's success.

Explain *How* to Change

Often when managers are bold and bring to someone's attention a concern, they feel like their job is done. However, we make the mistake of telling people WHAT they need to change, but not HOW. For example, if you tell someone on your team they need to have a more positive attitude, there's a good chance they'll agree with you. "Man, you're right. Even my spouse tells me my attitude sucks." You were straight. They agreed. Your job is done. However, if they knew HOW to have a more positive attitude, they'd already have one.

Help them by outlining the tangible steps they can take to shift their attitude. A good place to start is with specific examples of their negative attitude and alternative options. Share what helps you. Uncover core beliefs and suggest a shift in mindset. Ask the individual to ask others what works for them. Suggest searching for articles and videos that explain how to gain a positive attitude. Let them know you'll touch base in a couple of weeks to see what they've uncovered. Then check in.

Manage an Overdescriber

Take for example an overdescriber on your team. They drive everyone bonkers because a five-minute touch base expands into an energy sucking half-hour. This isn't the employee's intention, he doesn't understand. Overdescribers often go into too much detail in an effort to prove their worth and impress with their expertise, commitment or hard work. They seek reassurance.

In a one-on-one exchange: When someone starts getting into the weeds, interrupt them. Say something along the lines of, "Sam, I know you work hard and you're competent as well as thoughtful. While I know you want me to understand your entire process, I trust you and your choices. I don't need this detail. All I need to know is the project is on time."

Ask, "Can I share with you a blind spot I see?" Then upon an affirmative response, "Cool, I really appreciate you being open. Sometimes I avoid giving you the floor in meetings because what I believe should be a five-minute update tends to take you much longer. You don't need to explain or justify your choices. As a team we trust you and, in most cases, we just need to know what, not why. If we need to know more, we'll ask."

If they seemed miffed, give them a non-work related analogy. "Can I give you an analogy? If I asked you to bring a sugar-free dessert to the potluck, all I need to know is you're on it. I don't need to know all the different desserts you considered, that you tried Stevia, honey, palm sugar, and applesauce nor all the trials and tribulations you went through to get the right ingredient with the right measurement that worked with the rest of the ingredients. I don't need to know where you shopped to find the ingredients or who you consulted to figure out the best recipe. (Pause and smile.) I know your diligence. I know it will be delicious."

Help them figure out HOW to avoid this behavior in the future:

- **Just give us the high-level update:** "I made a sugar-free cake and had to try four sugar-free substitutes before I figured out what worked."

- **Code word:** Have a word you two agree upon that you can use to kindly interrupt when they're headed into the weeds.

- **Provide a honing tool:** Provide a one-page framework with a few questions to help narrow down what to share at the next meeting.

- **But not every employee can be guided to a better place.** Then you face the hard choice to do what's best for the organization.

Know When to Stop Investing in an Employee

There comes a time when you've done everything you can to make a square peg fit into a round hole. I'm all for compassion, empathy and understanding. However I'm also for what's best for your organization and the individuals you employ.

If you're not completely sure if the time has come to stop investing in an employee's development, consider asking the following:

1. Is the missing skill a need-to-have or a nice-to-have?

2. Have you clearly communicated the peg is square and the hole is round and it's not a good fit? Give specific examples. Before setting someone free, you must give an employee a real opportunity to improve. Be clear and honest in how the individual does and does not meet expectations. Be direct and let them know if the gap is job threatening.

3. Once approached, has the employee sought ways to address this gap?

4. How long has this person been square and the hole round?

5. Have you tried to change the shape of the hole to accommodate this team member? This is not a good sign. Find people to fill the position, not positions to fit the people.

6. Are there other areas in your organization where you have a square hole and need a square peg? If not, set them free to find an organization that needs a square peg.

7. How much time, energy and resources have you put toward trying to "transform" this individual? What are the concrete measurable outcomes of these efforts? What long-term changes or lack of changes have you witnessed?

8. On days when this person is giving you his best, is their performance at the level you need for this position? If you answered no, this person is not right for the position. Unfortunately a square peg can have the best intentions to fit into a round hole. They can try really hard. They might even find a way to wedge in a bit. But if they don't fit, they don't fit.

Fire Toxic Rainmakers

On the character side, nothing erodes a leader's credibility faster than a toxic individual who remains on the team due to their "amazing" talent. They cause internal drama and frustration. They treat fellow co-workers rudely, knowing they can get away with it. They're entitled prima donnas. No one can stand them, and yet everyone accommodates them, because you do.

You set what's acceptable, what's valued, what's rewarded.

I know this, because I've been there. I've been the CEO who feels I have an "untouchable." An employee I think our team can't live without. My company suffered for my lack of vision, my lack of spine, and my refusal to put the team before the superstar. I lost the respect of my team.

Until I saw my blind spot. The moving company was bigger than any single individual. All of us relied on it to provide not only income, but meaning to our lives. I saw that no single employee has the power to make or break my company. I finally opened my eyes to the brutal emotional and financial impact of this employee's negativity, negativity I had permitted for too long.

Often I have clients who feel like they are held captive by an employee's extraordinary expertise, sales capability, industry connections, longevity in the company, or iron-clad employment contract, among other reasons.

Instead, consider:

- If this person were gone tomorrow, you and your team would rally and figure it out. You're successful because you're resourceful.

- The negative impact this individual has on the rest of your employees' productivity, loyalty and morale is far more expensive than any financial gain they create.

- You don't even know the half of it. People stopped coming to you with their concerns long ago.

- They are not nearly as fabulous and valuable as you think they are. Really, I promise.

- Most of your people think you're either blind or an idiot for keeping this jerk. They can't fathom why you put up with such behavior.

- You're not blind and you're not an idiot. Do what needs to be done. Now.

Be Intolerant to Improve Your Culture

"Culture change is a double-or-nothing deal. When leaders don't hold themselves and others accountable for living up to stated values, they make a bad situation worse. They create a schizophrenic organization ruled by duplicity, contempt and cynicism."

—Fred Kofman, philosopher and Vice President of LinkedIn.

What is unacceptable in your organization? What is intolerable?

- Verbal abuse
- Intimidation by a manager or co-worker
- Continued disregard and disrespect for procedures
- Territorialism and lack of willingness to collaborate
- Throwing people under the bus
- Passive aggressive comments in meetings
- Consistent lack of follow through on commitments

Intolerance doesn't require pounding your fist on the table. In fact, it is the quiet, clear, grounded intolerance that speaks volumes.

Communicate both what you're a stand for and what you're a stand against.

Imagine if someone on your leadership team makes an insensitive comment. Stop the conversation. Pause. Look them in the eye *with compassion and conviction,* and say, "Mary, I know in the past when you've made comments like this I've given passive permission by grimacing and chuckling. The truth is it makes me uncomfortable. I'm not okay with this type of language in our organization. We say we value respect and it's just not in alignment with who we say we are."

Being intolerant marshals what it means to be a part of this team. Not just anybody gets to play. There's a pride that goes along with being a worthy member of a tribe.

I worked with one client and we came up with a short list of what they don't tolerate:

- Prima donnas

- Blame

- Grudges

- Gossip

- Pretense

- Know-it-alls

- Stiffs

- Micromanagement

- Stigma of remote workers

- Us vs. Them

What's your list?

Stop Workplace Bullying

Be a stand against workplace bullying. Don't minimize it. Don't turn away. This is more than a workplace issue.

When a 31-year-old firefighter-paramedic took her life in 2016, her employer uncovered that on-the-job bullying and harassment likely contributed to her duress.

First, understand what workplace bullying is.

Workplace bullying does not include feeling upset or unappreciated. Constructive feedback can hurt our feelings. So can being demoted or dismissed. Uncomfortable conflict and disagreements are not bullying (in fact these can be quite healthy.)

We also know the team that ribs each other mercilessly, laughs and bonds over the experience. While it's a pattern of behavior some might find offensive, in this case there's no malicious intent. The intent is to connect.

Workplace bullying on the other hand weaves together two vicious factors: a repetitive pattern of behavior and malicious intent.

Examples of repetitive patterns of bullying behavior include:

- Mocking, ridiculing or belittling
- Harshly teasing
- Yelling or screaming
- Condescending comments
- Vicious gossip
- Threatening words or gestures
- "Icing" someone out
- Withholding information
- Staring or glaring

The impact of these behaviors is intensified when done in front of others. Single instances of these types of behavior should be addressed immediately so they are not allowed to become patterns.

Malicious intent includes the desire to:

- Intimidate
- Degrade or demean
- Sabotage
- Socially isolate
- Defame character
- Retaliate
- Vilify
- Humiliate

Be vigilant and curious when claims of bullying present themselves. Don't make assumptions about either individual. Ask questions and listen carefully for intent. Consider if there's a power differential. Make sure no one is looking to shift focus from an underlying issue such as a lack of performance.

Listen and hold space for the truth to present itself.

Shifting your team's perception of traditional blaming accountability to the "ability to count" and "workable integrity" is essential for laying the foundational empowering context to talk about performance success and struggles. When someone is struggling, renounce unkind niceness and be a stand for their success. Help them see how to shift. If the shift doesn't occur, be decisive. Set free those individuals who are not a good fit. It's the compassionate, kind next step for them and for the team. Lastly, hold fast to your high standards, and your team's trust. Your culture depends on it.

Chapter 7

Build Trust and Break Down Division

- Grant Your Trust

- Trust Intentions

- Know the Types of Trust

- Eliminate Witch Hunts

- Shatter the Boss Stereotype

- Wipe the Slate Clean

- Shed Old Baggage

- Quell Generational Drama

- Go Speed Dating

- Enhance Virtual Workplace Camaraderie

Supervisor   **Co-workers**   **Autonomy**   **Organizational Support**   **Organizational Fit**

"The best way to find out if you can trust somebody is to trust them."

—Ernest Hemingway, novelist and journalist

To trust someone is to believe them, to have confidence they will tell you the truth and be reliable. This doesn't seem like such a tall order, and yet it is. We hesitate to trust. We don't want to be fools. Throw in the mix two groups and sameness loyalty can start cleaving us versus them. Doubt lingers. Betrayal is awaited. We see this in the workplace all the time. Leadership vs. staff. Old school vs. new school. On-site vs. virtual. Instill and inspire trust to unify the chasms. Here's how...

Grant Your Trust

During my presentation about the importance of trust at the McCombs Business School at the University of Texas, a man raised his hand with a challenge.

"Trust, trust, trust, that's the new buzz word. And that's all nice and good, but in real life I have to micromanage my team and watch their every move because at the end of the day, if it doesn't get done, it's my butt on the line," he said.

"Do you trust me if I don't trust you?" I asked.

"No."

"Would you provide your best work for someone who doesn't trust you?"

"No."

"If you don't trust your employees. They won't trust you and they are then unlikely to do their best work for you, which will then require your micromanagement efforts. It's a self-fulfilling prophecy." He thoughtfully paused, sat back down and took it in.

We trust people who trust us. We respect people who respect us.

(We also like people who like us.)

In our society we often say with hand on hip, "You've gotta earn my trust." Let's flip that. Consider applying to your workplace our legal system's presumption of "innocent until proven guilty." It's an ideal that dates back to the Romans, so I'd say it has stood the test of time.

Assuming you have done your due diligence to check references and do background checks, you should trust a new employee until they prove themselves untrustworthy. Trust they have a good work ethic. Trust they want to do their best. By giving your trust, you communicate you believe in them.

Will you get burned on occasion? Yes. But it's rare.

Live and lead for what's probable.

For employees well past orientation, trust their ability in how to get the work done. Remember, our research indicated that one of the eight critical factors that makes employees feel good about coming to work is autonomy. Clarify expectations, define critical boundaries, encourage questions when they get stuck and then let them run with the task. Trust their ability to lead their own work. Autonomy results from trust and spurs pride, ownership, self confidence and creative problem solving.

The next time an employee comes to you with a quandary, ask them, "Well, what do you think?" Listen, and as often as possible, empower their confidence and pluck by responding, "Sounds like a good option, go try it out and let me know how it goes."

Trust Intentions

Intent speaks to someone's heart, their deliberate purpose. When you question someone's intent, you question the core of their character. When you judge someone's intent, you knife their character:

- "He's just in it for himself."

- "She's power hungry."

- "She doesn't care about the project, she's just here for a paycheck."

- "He's just sucking up to the boss."

When intentions are perceived to be anything but pure, the judged feel hurt and resulting indignation seep into the space. A simple disagreement about strategy and tactics transforms into something personal and insurmountable.

The gulf escalates from "While I know Joe and I have the same end game in mind, I disagree with his method" to "He's a jerk who doesn't care."

Check out these two walruses. They could spend hours bickering and berating, even though they're both right. All it

would take is for one of them to invite the other to come to her side to see her perspective. She could also take the initiative to waddle over to the other side and simply ask, "Can you help me understand what you see?" This is trusting intentions. Stay curious and seek to understand.

If your team believes everyone, in their heart of hearts, is doing the best they can to accomplish the shared mission, then disagreements are simply that—disagreements, not personal attacks.

One of my clients holds close the value "Assume Positive Intent." Yet, with this value in place, one of their long-time employees stole from the organization. Background checks had been done, processes were followed, checks and balances were in place. This was simply an anomaly by one dishonest person who knew the system well. The betrayal horrified leadership. The public reputation implications were significant and painful.

Leadership was tempted to "make an example" of this person and to implement additional checks and balances. A culture of suspicion and distrust was close at hand. "Assume Positive Intent" was gasping for life.

I then reminded leadership, "Your people feel just as betrayed as you do. Everyone in your organization cares about your mission and works hard every day to serve your clients. They are equally angry this individual undermined their hard work and the organization's reputation. When the story hits the newspapers, they, too, will need to explain the situation to their friends and family."

Leadership decided to hold off on those additional checks and balances. They had a trustworthy team. But they also paused to examine the bottom line implications—implementing triple checking would cost ten dollars to save fifty cents.

During rough times, hold fast to your faith in your team and your core values. It will come back to you tenfold as your team puts their faith in you and in the organization.

Know the Types of Trust

We trust people who trust us. The reverse is true. We don't trust those who don't. When we feel someone doesn't trust us, it's insulting. It's a dagger through the heart of our character. We become indignant, defensive and distant. Next time "I don't trust you" is about to fall out of your mouth, stop.

Moderate your language. Speak to your specific concern, challenge or need. Not your trust.

Think about what kind of trust you are questioning:

- **Work Ethic**—I trust you will carry your own weight and work hard.
- **Competency**—I trust you have the capacity and ability to do your job well.
- **Humility**—I trust you know your limits and will ask for help and guidance when you need it.
- **Ethics**—I trust you'll do the right thing.
- **Self Accountability**—I trust that if you make a mistake you'll own it and won't shift the blame.
- **Intentions**—I trust you are trying to do what's best for the organization as a whole.
- **Integrity**—I can count on you to do what you say you will do.
- **Honesty and Transparency**—I trust you're telling the truth and not lying by omission.
- **Thoughtfulness**—I trust you to consider the impact on others of your decisions and actions.
- **Alliance**—I trust you to have my back.
- **What Happens in Vegas**—I trust you will keep this in the utmost confidence.
- **Vulnerability**—I trust you won't judge me when I share personal challenges.

I had a client who was really concerned one of her key leadership team members didn't trust anyone. He often said, "We don't have to trust each other. I just want everyone to do their job."

Instead of falling prey to her assumption, she asked him which level of trust he was referring to. He responded, "We don't have to trust each other with our inner-most secrets [Vulnerability], I just want to trust I can count on everyone to follow through on their responsibilities [Integrity]." She breathed a sigh of relief realizing they were on the same page.

When you look at this list, in what areas do you trust your team? In what areas don't you? Do you have reasons? Cite specific examples. If you don't have specific examples, and barring the last three on the list, your trust issues could have more to do with you than your team.

Eliminate Witch Hunts

When something goes wrong, often the first question is "Who did it?" The blame game and the witch hunt ensue. It becomes a bloodbath.

Employees trust and feel safe when they can fail. Create a safe space. Be committed to continuous improvement. View mistakes as an opportunity for learning and growth. When "it" hits the fan, start with "Help me understand..." Seek solutions. "How did we get here?" "What do we need to do to avoid this in the future?"

Consider creating something like the "Confessional Gong."

Neenan, a progressive architecture and construction company, has a large brass gong that hangs in their meeting room. During a company

meeting, if someone has made a mistake—cost the company money, caused conflict on the team, jeopardized a project opportunity—they go to the front of the room and share what they did, what they learned, apologize and then strike the gong.

Neenan employees often earn praise and admiration from their co-workers for having courage to own their mistakes. What's most powerful

about this process is *every person in the room learns from their peer's mistake.*

I asked one employee, "Tell me, has there ever been a time in a review when your supervisor said, 'You know, you've hit that gong just a few too many times.'"

"Never."

Management knows the tremendous benefit of this practice and knows not to jeopardize this foundation of trust, honesty and openness.

Key to the success of this experience is the CEO's own demonstration of humility when he stands squarely before his team, picks up the mallet and strikes the gong, his acknowledgment of error reverberating throughout the room.

Shatter the Boss Stereotype

"At the end of the game, the king and the pawn go back in the same box."

—**Italian proverb** written above the CEO's office at DaVita

You have an open door policy, but nobody tells you anything. You hear concerns through the grapevine or from one of your internal trusted advisors. You ask for feedback from your team, yet you get zilch. Why won't they talk to me?

Consider, do you:

- Give off an air of being too busy or seem impatient?
- Have your office door closed often?
- Struggle to keep confidences or talk about employees with other employees?
- Take things personally?
- Demonstrate intimidating or condescending body language?

If you answer no to all of the above, then chances are you're boxed in a "boss" stereotype.

Societally we are told bosses are:

- Greedy
- Power hungry
- Stupid or clueless
- Egotistical
- Insensitive

Just think about common sitcoms and comics that leverage this stereotype:

- The Simpsons
- The Office
- Dilbert
- SpongeBob
- Parks & Recreation

Many work teams bond over disdain for "the boss." You've seen it, a knowing glance or under-the-breath, "just between you and me" comment to a co-worker. A team's commitment to "us vs. the boss" can feel soul crushing and impossible to overcome.

The only way to move past deep-rooted beliefs about bosses is to share your humanity.

As a leader, you're expected to set the example, be fearless and confidently guide the team through challenging times. Yet you're a real deal human being, warts and all. You have insecurities. You make mistakes. You don't have all the answers. Sometimes you question your own judgment.

Many supervisors have *not* been mentored to show humility, demonstrate vulnerability or share insecurities. Showing these can feel even more difficult when your team buys into the boss stereotype. You *need* to be vulnerable.

Your team needs to know you bleed just like they do.

When they do, they will share with you their concerns and challenges. They will be right there, fighting beside you.

A few years back I was working with a team that managed a line of retail stores. As we were processing the Culture Audit™ survey comments our team at Choose People made a startling discovery: The organization's second in command, a man close to the CEO, had become "Public Enemy Number One" in the staff's eyes. They would mock his mannerisms and spread horror stories behind his back. They even gave him a twisted nickname—Voldemort, after the ghastly, inhuman evil of the Harry Potter films. They had bonded over their shared contempt for him.

The complaints against him stretched out for pages and even detailed very specific threats of physical violence against him that I won't bother to share here—but feel free to use your imagination.

They certainly did.

The staff's united hatred of this man was such a powerful presence in the organization but neither he nor the management knew anything about it. The CEO, the leadership team and even the HR department were stunned at the devastating revelation. He was tight enough to the CEO that he wasn't going to lose his job but things were bad.

So the question was how to turn around this culture of hatred against him?

"Voldemort" had one choice. Own his behavior. Apologize.

He did. He went to his team, hat in hand, and said, "I'm so sorry... I had no idea this was your experience of me." He reflected their concerns and spoke to how he would change his ways.

They gave him a standing ovation. In that moment, he transformed from boss to human.

Wipe the Slate Clean

If distrust is rampant in your organization you need to wipe the slate clean. I see many organizations hope "it'll just go away with time." It doesn't. It festers.

As the head honcho, you must apologize to the team. Describe in detail how the organization got here. Make eye contact, and pause to emphasize you truly understand how serious and painful the situation has been for the team. Describe what it looks like and feels like and be frank:

> "We went through hell during the recession and furloughed a lot of people. People many of you considered not only colleagues, but also friends. We said that when the economy turned around we would hire them back. We haven't. Rumor has it that we're not going to.
>
> There is another rumor the leadership team doesn't care about these people and that we only care about making a profit. The truth is part of the rumor is correct. We're not going to hire them back. I want to apologize for giving them, as well as many of you, false hope. You have to know it's not because we don't care.
>
> The feedback we received on our employee survey indicates you're comfortable with your workload. The business reality is we simply don't need additional people.
>
> This doesn't mean we don't care. We do care. Furloughing loyal, committed employees was brutal. We hope to never do it again. Should another recession hit, we want everyone in this room to continue to be here."

This one act alone—done authentically—allows leadership to regain the credibility critical for sustainable forward progress.

Now keep in mind, you only get one chance to apologize and create a clean slate. ONLY say it if you mean it.

If you're thinking, "Really, is this necessary? They just need to move on." They won't. Step up and apologize. It is the only path forward.

Shed Old Baggage

Does your organization have baggage? Or rather, mistakes from the past that individuals on your team dredge up on a semi-regular basis? Do you wonder why won't they let it go?

There are several possible reasons:

- They've been told to "move on," "just let it go," or "get over it." Heels dig deep.

- Old wounds make for an easy scapegoat.

- Baggage is evidence to avoid change. We tried to innovate and look at what happened.

- The old guard wants to be recognized for their loyalty, strength and grit, to be acknowledged for having gotten the organization to where it is today. They have lived to tell to the tale. And they will tell it, over and over again.

- The skeletons were never truly laid to rest. They have not been forgiven and will not be forgotten.

Old baggage that hangs around fouling the culture is deadly for an organization. If your employees continue to bring the poisonous past into the unspoiled present, your future will repeat the past. There will be little progress. New employees come in bright-eyed and bushy-tailed. Within weeks, reality checks from their disgruntled counterparts crush their rose-colored glasses.

Baggage is never too old to shed. If a mistake, a miscalculated strategy or a layoff wasn't handled well and the aftermath wasn't acknowledged, the baggage is still haunting your organization. It needs to be addressed.

 Action Jackson:
Release Old Baggage

With your whole team together:

1. **Describe the gory details of what happened.** Really. Everyone already knows them. They want to know YOU know them.

2. **Do not explain why** the issue was handled the way it was (this hasn't worked before and it's not going to work now.) It makes you appear defensive and sounds like an "I'm sorry, but..."

3. **Acknowledge the impact of the issue.** While you're over it, they're not. Take this up a notch. The impact was deeper than you think or it's gained depth as the pain of time has carved into the organization. Speak to how hard it was for everyone.

4. **Apologize.** If you were part of leadership when the issue was created, own the issue. If you weren't, apologize on behalf of those who were. It is much easier to forgive and forget when a genuine apology has been offered.

5. **Recognize and thank those who endured.** Appreciate their contribution in getting the organization where it is today.

6. **Speak to the future in your *next* all team meeting.** Do not address it during this gathering or it will feel like everything that came before wasn't genuine.

Share:

- In our last meeting, I spoke to several tough challenges we've faced in the past.

- Today, we are up to great things. We can't allow past mistakes to hold us back.

- I'd like *to ask* all of you who went through that awful time to let go of the past and help create an exciting present and future for us all to live into.

Meaningfully paint the picture of the future.

Then ask: "Please stand up (or raise your hand) if you're on board." You want physically demonstrated agreement. Pause and survey the room, making kind eye contact with each individual.

What if they don't respond? There are no guarantees, but every time I have made this recommendation, the entire team stands. The peer pressure and peer support for a better future overrides the stubborn. Within days of this second meeting, rehashing past baggage becomes passé. Grace, forgiveness and a clean slate lighten the space.

Intervention works both as an antidote to a poisonous past and a balm to generational division.

Quell Generational Drama

Do you have inter-generational drama? Especially between Boomers and Millennials?

Ageism is common. This cuts `both ways. Consider the stereotypical off-hand comments, "Millennials are entitled," or "Old people are clueless." In the company of people of a similar age, corroboration is forthcoming. Too often, ageism is a socially accepted scapegoat for why people choose not to work well together.

We reject those who judge our character without knowing us.

However the root cause of ageism, other than the righteous ego hit of "we're better than them," can often be found in our ability to relate. Our age reflects where we are in our life cycle whether it's renting our first apartment, dating, getting married, buying a home, having children, or taking care of parents and grandkids. For individuals at different stages, more effort is required to relate.

I had coffee with a bright 24-year-old who likes his job and enjoys where he works. However sometimes he struggles to relate since he's the youngest on the team by a decade. He's living with his parents and trying to figure out the balance of health, work, adventure and partying. He said he went to lunch with some of his work colleagues and tried not to roll his eyes when they started comparing backyard landscaping.

"I don't even have a home, let alone a backyard I would want to spend time landscaping," he said.

I suggested next time he meets with his co-workers to try asking about their lives:

- Where were they in the world when they were 24?

- What's one piece of advice they'd give to their 24-year-old selves?

- What's the most unusual item on their bucket list?

- How do they balance work, health and play?

Another key source of contention between Millennials and Boomers is a perceived lack of respect. Boomers want to be valued for their hard-earned expertise while Millennials are less likely to respect someone *simply* due to position, title or knowledge. There's a sense these are over-rated. You can find knowledge on Google or learn how on YouTube.

Millennials do value (as we all do) those who are interested, invested and involved. They seek personal and professional growth and appreciate those who share their experiences of learning. They value true connection.

Millennials also want to know "why" not because they're questioning someone's intelligence or authority, but because they want to learn. They want to understand the reasoning backing a decision.

Add to the mix new technology. Often Boomers' confidence and wisdom is undermined by trying to "find the damn document that used to be housed over here." Nobody likes feeling stupid. It's incredibly demoralizing to go from being the "go-to" expert of the old system to the novice of the new one. Younger individuals are often unaware of how their fluidity with navigating technology and speed at absorbing information leaves others behind.

So you have Boomers feeling disrespected calling Millennials entitled and Millennials rolling their eyes at their slow counterparts. To break down this disunity, first and foremost, stand on common ground. Focus on what they have in common rather than where they diverge.

Then foster more empathy and connection through these next two Action Jacksons.

 ### Action Jackson:
Team Generational Conversation

Bring the team together and speak to the importance of age diversity. Speak to how ingenuity is fostered through the lens of differing perspectives. Talk through the following ways to demonstrate humility and respect, regardless of age:

- Acknowledge if you have less experience or comfort on a topic and freely admit when you don't know something.
- Validate one another's contribution and openly admire skills and knowledge.
- Include one another in conversations and seek advice and feedback.
- Seek to understand the others' perspective and be empathetic.
- Be curious about one another and find common ground—share stories, past experiences, aspirations.

- Never be dismissive or condescending.

- Assume it's NOT because of your age.

- Reach out to someone from another generation with the intention to learn both about and from one another.

These could apply to bringing together other factions, however these are particularly helpful with breaking down ageism.

 Action Jackson:
Go Speed Dating

I'm often asked for team building exercises. While many are lackluster or forced fun, this one has never failed:

1. Print the questions outlined below—one set for each participant.

2. Have everyone stand and pair up, ideally with someone they don't know well. If there are an odd number of people, it's okay to have a threesome.

3. Give instructions:

   a. Each couple will have a total of three minutes together.

   b. You can start with any question you want.

   c. You can cover all five questions or just one.

   d. When I yell STOP, high five your partner.

   e. Then switch and find a new partner.

   f. We'll do three rounds.

   g. GO! Then use your timer.

The room will get progressively loud, full of smiles and laughter.

I've included two sets of questions in case you want to run more than three rounds. Run the first set of questions for the first three rounds, and the second set of questions for the last three rounds. The reason for the second set of questions is simply to keep the dialogue fresh. Of course feel free to create your own questions!

First Set

1. What would your friends or family say you're known for?

2. What's the most common misperception people have of you?

3. Find three things you two have in common.

4. In 60 seconds tell your life story in as much detail as possible.

5. Share an embarrassing or inspiring moment in your life.

Second Set

1. What's something you've done that has taken you out of your comfort zone?

2. What's your favorite childhood memory?

3. What do you consider "paradise"?

4. What was your biggest challenge last year?

5. What's your favorite gift you've ever received/given?

Here's the kicker, those who have partnered up will not have enough time to fully answer all of the questions, leaving them with a thread to pick up at a later time. "Hey, didn't you say you have a puppy? I'm thinking of getting one too, any suggestions? Oh and I never did get to hear your favorite childhood memory..."

There will also be those who didn't pair up who now have questions to better understand one another. "Hey, you and I didn't get to connect. I'm curious, what is an inspiring moment from your life?"

....

Enhance Virtual Workplace Camaraderie

Becoming more prevalent is the division between mixed office and virtual teams. And unfortunately, the speed dating exercise isn't helpful. So let's talk about how you and your remote teams can rock some serious camaraderie.

A note here, everything in this book is as mission critical to distributed work teams as it is for same physical space ones. However...

Distributed teams require more consistent intentional effort to create the feeling of being known, matter and included.

Otherwise your team can quickly go down the path of feeling neglected, unsupported and isolated.

Here's a few foundational keys to create virtual teams conducive to camaraderie:

1. **When hiring, evaluate for conversational aptitude.** How easy is it to carry a conversation with this person? Is there conversational chemistry? Is this person warm and easy to connect with?

2. **When hiring, evaluate for active listening aptitude.** Are they able to reflect back ideas you've conveyed or walk through steps you've outlined? Are they curious and ask thoughtful questions in response to what you've shared?

3. **When hiring, evaluate for being a self-starter.** Are their prior life choices intentional or one of happenstance? Do things happen to them or do they make things happen? Have they demonstrated being proactive in the interview process?

4. **Introduce new team members one at a time.** Schedule new employees to have 30-minute one-on-one video calls with each of the people they will work with on a regular basis. It's vital to put a name with a face and voice.

5. **Ideally keep teams to four or five individuals and no more than ten.** The fewer people, the more inclusive communication and the easier it is to schedule, align and coordinate the work.

6. **Require face-to-face proximity and courtesy.** Use video as often as possible for meetings and ask people to set up their camera as if they were sitting at a table across from their teammates. Make eye contact. No multi-tasking. Be present and honor one another's time.

7. **Task teams with a focused specific outcome or result.**

8. If possible, rather than giving them a task list (occurs more often in virtual teams), **have teams collaborate to figure out how to get the work done** based on their strengths and time available.

9. **Share facilitation.** If appropriate, take turns leading and facilitating discussions. Use a round robin approach to garner ideas from everyone. This leverages getting to know different people within a preexisting context.

Here's several easy ways to deepen connection (these work well in same space workplaces too):

- **Monday Morning Momentum:** If possible, have each small core team gather on a video call for a few minutes to share about their weekend and what they're looking to accomplish that week. This is a good time to leverage the "Cadence of Accountability" check-in as well.

- **Fun and Fast:** Take a deep dive on a team member's personal interest in five minutes. Have one team member follow the Ignite format of sharing their knowledge on a topic of their interest using 20 slides that auto-advance every 15 seconds. Examples at ignitetalks.io.

- **Connect Four:** Set the expectation that each team member is responsible for getting to know better four of their cohorts each month. Schedule 30-minute "getting to know all about you" exchanges. Pairs can lean on the Speed Dating questions if they need fodder.

- **Rose, Bud, Thorn:** Once a week, give everyone on the team three minutes at the beginning of the meeting to share their personal and professional Rose, Bud, Thorn on page 102.

- **Check Everyone's Temperature:** Details on page 102.

- **Show and Tell:** Have everyone give a video tour of their workplace. Or share their favorite meme or three items they'd save in a fire.

- **Celebrate Wins:** Play "We are the Champions" by Queen and belt out together "No time for losers, 'cause we are the champions of the wooooorld." Be goofy and try to high five one another.

- **Leverage Music:** While you may not be able to do a conga line or the cupid shuffle, you can do the chicken dance together via video. Or play the song "Jump" (Kriss Kross or Van Halen both work) and literally jump together.

- **Swap and Share:** Recipes. Coolest new app. Bucket lists. Your worst nightmare. Stress relief or time management tip. Favorite song.

- **Article Club:** Take turns sharing an *interesting* article that expands learning related to your work and have everyone read and discuss.

- **All Plaid Friday:** Or polka dot. Or ugly sweater. Or 70s. You get the idea.

- **JibJab:** Make a JibJab card for your team—super cheesy and it'll make them laugh.

- **Story Jam:** Pick a topic for the month and have everyone share a short story from their life. You can check out themoth.org for inspirational topics.

- **Bad Clean Jokes:** Probably the thing remote workers miss most from an office environment. What did the cop say to her stomach? You're underavest.

- **Friday Afternoon Club:** If possible, have everyone end the week by gathering for a few minutes to share the highlight of their week and what they're up to for the weekend.

Trust is reciprocal. To break down divisions and bring your team together, identify common ground and assume positive intent. Share your humanity and own the impact. Shatter stereotypes. Encourage camaraderie. And don't forget to invest in a confessional gong.

Five-Minute Favor: As someone who is deep into this book, you believe in human potential.

In an effort to encourage others to bring joy to their workplace, please review this book on Amazon.

Your review will move us one step closer to shifting the national conversation around work from one of woe to one of joy.

Chapter 8

Nurture Kind, Candid and Constructive Communication

- Dig Deeper

- Keep Employees in the Know

- Listen to the Breadcrumbs

- Encourage Candor through Public Praise

- Rein in Gossip

- Entwine Emotional and Professional

- Take Your Team's Temperature

- Open with Rose, Bud, Thorn

- Reduce a Culture of Comparison

- Take it Personally

| Supervisor | Co-workers | Organizational Support | Organizational Fit | Work-Family Climate |

"How we believe others see us shapes who we are. We ride a wave of pride or get swallowed in a sea of embarrassment based on brief interactions that signal respect or disrespect.... Civility lifts people. Incivility holds people down.

—Christine Porath, Professor of Management
at Georgetown University

Talk is cheap. Communication is priceless. Communication shows you care. Sharing, inquiring, listening and understanding are all ways to communicate and connect. Consistent, caring communication creates trust. Teams trust when they feel safe and in the loop. On the other hand, lack of communication sabotages culture with confusion, assumptions and rumors.

Dig Deeper

"We need better communication."

This is the catch-all scapegoat of organizations (and employee surveys). The facts back up the perception. A Salesforce.com study found that 86 percent of executives blame failures at their companies on a lack of collaboration and poor communication.

What does it really mean?

- I don't know what's going on.
- I don't feel I can voice my opinion.
- I don't trust one of my co-workers.
- I'm not appreciated for the work I do.
- There's too much gossip and bickering.
- I don't think our decision making process is fair.
- I want more support and guidance from my manager.

The next time someone says, "We need better communication," dig deeper. "Tell me more" is a great phrase. Get to specifics. Garner repeated examples. Then address those. Otherwise you're throwing darts in the dark.

Keep Employees in the Know

Surprises at work are unnerving. Eyebrows raise when there's an *unexpected addition or reduction* in staff, compensation, workload, product offerings, project scope or timing. The impact ranges from feeling miffed and annoyed to feeling blindsided and betrayed. Productivity plunges as employees try to regain their footing.

Shock is remembered. The next time they are less resilient.

Consistent, caring communication creates trust. Teams trust when they feel safe and in the loop. Transparency is easy during good times. However when sales dive, a competitor gains coveted ground or a client threatens to sue, leadership often retreats into silence. They withdraw behind closed conference room doors while distrust breeds among staff.

Closed doors seed and grow unseen mistrust. They are scary. They are emblematic of not knowing. I mentioned this during a presentation in Minneapolis. An executive from a large bank jumped out of her chair, and said "Oh my gosh, that's SO true! Just the other day I was in my office talking with Joy about which day would work best for the company meeting. We had the door closed. And we needed Mark's input. So we called him into my office and asked him which date would be better. And he said, 'Are you two just talking about the calendar?' We nodded yes. And I couldn't believe it. He literally walked out of my office and shouted out to the cubicles of employees: 'It's okay everybody, they're just talking about the calendar'."

In a culture of uncertainty, closing a door signals the sky is falling.

Your employees are smart. If you don't provide answers, they will turn over every rumor rock searching for them. If no facts are forth-coming they will invent what they believe to be true. Instead of creating fertile ground for distrust, share the pain. When you share dilemmas, your employees feel included.

Once briefed on the challenge, include them in problem solving. You can then rally your team's support and leverage their insight.

Provide monthly updates on the "State of the Union" in person or via video. Outline progress on quarterly goals. Speak to current financial health, successes, challenges, and what's being done about those challenges. Solicit questions from the team beforehand and speak to those directly.

Listen to the Breadcrumbs

As a manager, your people may be communicating more than you hear because they speak very, very softly.

George lightly knuckle knocks on your office door, peaks his head inside and asks,

"Hey do you have a second? Really, no big deal if you don't. Well okay, I just thought you might want to know Jimmy and Mary had a little spat this afternoon. Again I don't think it's that big of a deal. No, I wouldn't worry about it too much. Just thought you might want to know."

George is trying to tell you there are "Jimmy and Mary" made bombs in the building and he just witnessed the third explosion. It took guts for George to come to you. Your people will drop breadcrumbs to a trail that may seem insignificant. They will even tell you it's insignificant. What you have to realize is those crumbs lead to a loaf of bread. Hell, even to a whole bakery.

Encourage Candor through Public Praise

Encourage candor by praising behavior you want to see. The next time someone gives you a breadcrumb that leads to a loaf of bread, tell the team how appreciative you are. "I want to thank George. He came by my office the other day and made me aware of the need for relationship repair between the sales and manufacturing departments. Without his help, I'd still be in the dark, and you all would still be frustrated. George, I really value your courage in being a stand for the success of the team. Thank you."

The next time someone gives you constructive feedback, thank them in front of the team. "I want to thank Kelly. Just the other day she gave me some really good feedback—that when I use all caps in my e-mails it comes off as if I'm yelling. I had no idea that was the impact. I will make a concerted effort from here on out to unlock my caps. Kelly, I super appreciate you letting me know. Thank you."

Over time, your team will become more and more candid with you. Make sure you continue to keep an open attitude as the frequency increases. As a leader always be appreciative of feedback, but don't always feel you have to respond. Check in to see if it resonates or if you've heard this before.

Rein in Gossip

Let's face it, gossip is titillating. It's a hot mess. It's the car wreck we simultaneously cringe at and rubberneck to get a better look. Productivity be damned, we have morbid curiosity. So it is hard to end gossip once it's become a habit.

We all know gossip is toxic. I once read in a spiritual text, "Backbiting extinguishes the light of the soul." DEEP. It does.

What often gets missed is why people gossip. It is rare for a person to gossip simply to be mean. Gossip occurs for one of four reasons:

1. **People crave intimacy and a sense of connection.**

    > *Gossip is one of the quickest and easiest ways to emotional intimacy. The secrecy, forbidden and exclusive nature of confiding something subversive or judgmental is social super glue.*

    Through the veneer of momentary vulnerability and trust, there's bonding. Unfortunately gossip is a sloppy second to real deal, meaningful connection. It's cheap, it's mean and it plays us small.

2. **People want to work with those they perceive as peers.** Shared competency matters. If someone you choose for your team isn't carrying their weight, isn't competent or isn't a good culture fit, there will be gossip. An underperformer or rude co-worker threatens the identity and pride of the team. Rather than being a "narc," employees will gossip behind his back not only about him but about leadership's lack of awareness and action. The longer you fail to deal with the situation, the nastier and more embedded the gossip becomes.

3. **People fear the unknown.** If people don't have the information they want, they will ask others, especially if that information appears to be hidden. This is why closed-door conversations can be so harmful. They breed inaccurate and often harmful assumptions.

4. **People want to belong and to be included.** The easiest way to identify those who are in the inner circle is to determine who's

in the know. Information is power. People who aren't given information aren't included and will seek the inside scoop.

So how do you reduce gossip?

Be transparent. Communicate where the organization is headed and the opportunities, challenges and obstacles on that road. Share the strategic plan (page 35). Share the financials with your team (page 40). Be clear how your employees plug into the strategy and how they impact the bottom line.

Be consistent in your communication and your actions. Secrets, unwritten rules, hypocrisy and un-communicated motives are a sure-fire way to have employees wonder if they know the whole truth.

Seek employee input and feedback before and during any significant organizational change. Whenever possible, include employees in decision-making. Take employee suggestions and concerns seriously and make sure to complete the response loop by communicating actions taken as a result of their input.

Provide real opportunities for people to connect, share and learn about one another. One of the most natural ways to do this is cross-departmental project work. If that isn't realistic in your organization, try something like a May Madness foosball tournament or check out the camaraderie building ideas from the previous chapter on pages 91–93.

Promptly address employees who are not performing. As a manager you have the unique honor and responsibility to guide, coach and support your team to being the best they can be. When an individual on the team is struggling to fit, whether it's a competency issue or a character issue, address it as soon as possible. Your team is watching and waiting.

Entwine Emotional and Professional

Real relationships require emotions. For years we've been told to separate our personal lives from our professional lives. We've been told to separate our emotions from our work. And we've tried, resulting in flat smiles, ill-fitting masks and just-below-the-surface passive aggressive tension.

Emotions are information. They should not be suppressed or disregarded. They tell you when something feels "right" or "off." They tell you when you're being true to yourself and when you're bluffing. You want to know if someone on your team is elated. You want to know if someone is frustrated or disappointed.

Encourage your employees to bring their whole selves to work, emotions and all. Along with their emotions comes their innovative problem-solving. There are times it's appropriate to feel frustration, sadness or guilt. When it's safe to express these emotions, growth, discovery and solutions flourish.

Recent research by the London Business School shows that employees who feel welcome to express their authentic selves at work exhibit higher levels of organizational commitment, individual performance, and propensity to help others.

Remember, emotions are contagious. Which works great if joy is in the air, not so great if apathy is spreading. Don't let them go unchecked. Get them out on the table.

How do you find out how your employees are *really* feeling? Your "open door policy" simply won't get you there. You have to ask. Unfortunately you can't just ask, "How are you doing?" You will only garner the socially-accepted and pat responses of:

- Fine.
- Good.
- Pretty good.
- Not too bad.
- Alright.
- Just another day in paradise.
- Livin' the dream.

You know nothing more than when you first asked the question. Try these two next Action Jacksons instead.

Action Jackson:
Take Your Team's Temperature

With the Temperature Check you can quickly track morale progress or decline. You will uncover both challenges to address and successes to acknowledge. Once this process becomes habitual, your team will be more thoughtful in, and accountable to, their responses. Inconsistency becomes self-evident when someone answers "eight" and then kvetches to a co-worker.

1. On a scale of 1–10 how are you doing this week?

   Note, usually 7 is indicative of "fine." Not lovin' it, not hatin' it. Less than 7 is usually concerning while more than 7 suggests the individual is truly in a "good space." Keep in mind, for your analytical types, 5 is "fine."

2. What contributes to that number? This question allows for discovery without judgment. Here is where you learn if their response is based on personal or professional conditions or a combo.

3. If it's six or higher, ask, what would make it a plus one?

4. If it's five or lower, ask, is there anything I can do to support you?

5. When the number is higher or lower than last time, ask, "What shifted?"

Action Jackson:
Open with Rose, Bud, Thorn

Open your next meeting with a round robin of Rose, Bud, Thorn. Have each team member take one minute to share:

- Rose: Best thing that's happened in the last week.
- Bud: What you're most looking forward to in the coming week.
- Thorn: Biggest challenge in the coming week.

   By the way, this is a great exercise to lead check-ins with your kids.
   (For clarity, this is not my idea. Unfortunately, I don't know who to attribute this exercise to as my daughter shared it with me and I was unable to uncover the author.)

Reduce a Culture of Comparison

Do you have someone on your team who is prone to comparison and scorekeeping? Have you heard this:

It's not fair:

- She gets paid more than I do.
- He got promoted and I didn't.
- She has a flexible work schedule and I don't.
- Their supervisor brings in burritos on Friday mornings and you don't.
- He got a new computer and I didn't.

If so, as a manager, you have two steps to take.

Step 1: Support your team member in taking personal responsibility for what they can control.

- If you want more pay, demonstrate an increase in your return on investment and then ask for a raise.
- If someone gets promoted and you don't, inquire into the factors that went into the decision. Evaluate what you need to do to be a top candidate.
- If your position doesn't allow for flexible hours and this is important to you, apply for a position that does.
- If you want burritos on Friday, ask if we, too, have a burrito budget.
- If you need a new computer to improve your work, request one.

Key point to impart here: Do not blame your co-worker. Rather wish the best for your co-worker, including good pay, a promotion, flexible work hours, burritos and a new computer. We're in this together. Together we create our daily work experience and share in contributing to the mission of this organization. We should stand for one another's success and wish well upon each other.

Step 2: Be just, not fair.

Don't try to make it fair, because you can't. Nobody has the same life experience. It will never be equal, or the same, or fair. It can however, be just.

- Share how compensation is determined.
- Share the decision factors that go into promotions and how those factors are weighed.
- When hiring, share the different inherent benefits and challenges of each position.
- Share if there's a flex team budget for each department.
- Share the criteria that necessitates the purchase of a new computer.

Comparisons and scorekeeping are rooted in a lack of understanding. If an employee sees how and why a decision is made, they may still wish things were different, but **they no longer make others wrong for having what they want.** When they understand how and why someone received a promotion, a new computer, or a flexible work schedule, they understand the equation and are empowered to make it happen for themselves.

Take it Personally

When someone gives you "constructive" feedback, it's personal.

When someone suddenly takes you off a pet project, it's personal.

When someone questions your motives, it's personal.

We're told not to take things personally, especially in the workplace. I suggest instead you **take it to heart**, especially if it's tough to hear. **Feel the sting.** Don't react. Don't run. Don't hide. Don't justify and defend. Just see if it uncomfortably resonates.

If it does, **thank the person** for their candor and change your attitude or behavior. To gain clarity on how to move forward, you may want to ask this individual, or those who stand for your success, "What would a shift look like?"

If it doesn't resonate, lead with curious inquiry rather than an accommodating apology. Ask for more clarity, "Help me understand, why is this your experience of me? What am I missing?" You can always let them know you don't see what they see, that while it doesn't resonate you're willing to try it on over the next few weeks and will circle back.

Many would tell you just to "let it go." The truth is, we don't. We fester. We close off. We fake. We may even obsess. Until you've actually considered the potential validity of what's been posed, you can't let it go. So consider it. Respond thoughtfully.

I had a close colleague tell me she didn't know if I really cared. I was horrified—me? Not care? How's that possible? I'm Choose People people!

I did the "right" thing by my internal accommodator and I apologized. Though I really couldn't believe it. I apologized even though I wasn't sorry. I wanted off the hook, without considering the validity. Then I mentally obsessed and defended some more. I was mad, how could she think this of me? I care. I care a lot. I was sad, frustrated. This was personal.

To ground myself, I leaned on vulnerability expert Brené Brown's advice, "choose discomfort over resentment." It wasn't until I confessed to not understanding her perspective that I was able to move forward. "What would it look like for you to know I cared?" I asked.

She said, "You tend to go silent between seeing one another. All it would take is a quick check in—perhaps a text, a quick e-mail, or message me on Facebook."

I knew she was right. I pride myself on being present to those who are in front of me, which also means those who aren't can feel forgotten. While I'm still no rockstar at check-ins, I'm better. I'm better both because she was willing to go there with me and because I took it personally.

And remember...

When someone praises you, it's personal.

When someone promotes you, it's personal.

When you're asked to head up a project, it's personal.

In closing, communication is the foundation to feeling safe. Healthy workplace communication means surprises are rare while change is explained. Emotions are encouraged while gossip is prohibited. Assumptions are uncommon while questions are commonplace. Self-awareness is applauded while comparison is quashed. Only under these conditions can emotional intimacy thrive.

Chapter 9

Repair Relationships

- Envision the Relationship Matrix

- Know Conflict Styles

- Understand How People Get to Funkytown

- Uncover the Source of the Relationship Breakdown

- Why We Stay in Funkytown

- Caution: Sneaky Sounding Boards

- Take Four Steps Out of Funkytown

- Conflict Resolution Between Two Employees

Supervisor   **Co-workers**   **Organizational Support**   **Organizational Fit**

"You must love truth more than you love saving face."

—Fred Kofman, philosopher and Vice President at Linkedin

Bear hug conflict. Embrace that elephant. Then lead him out of the building. Because if you just wait it out, hope it just goes away, a whole family of elephants will spawn and rampage through your workplace. This chapter will cover how relationships break down into Funkytown and how you can get out of there with grace.

For clarity, this work isn't theoretical. I know this work well as I've been at the center of many a Funkytown experience. Remember the beef jerky? Or the friend where I had to take it personally? For the record, here's me embracing another elephant:

Mouth, insert foot. I saw her face drop. I had complimented one of my key employees at the moving company on her new ring. Proudly she shared how she shrewdly haggled a street vendor while on vacation in Mexico. Her coup de grâce was she cried to get the price she wanted. I was horrified. Incredulous I said, "Are you kidding me?" My harsh judgment splattered all over her. Enter Funkytown.

We stayed there a few days. I wasn't sure I could repair this relationship. I was her boss and I demeaned an experience she was proud of in her personal life. How would she ever open up to me again? Not to mention I still had the judgmental voice in my head questioning her manipulation. After some self-reflection, I got a clue. I invited her to a conversation. I shared a bit of my history that would shed light on why I was triggered. I also shared that this was no excuse. I apologized for what I said and the impact it had on her. While it took some time for her trust in me to fully revive, the elephant was not left to feed on our awkward silence.

Envision the Relationship Matrix

Imagine you're sitting across from a co-worker, any co-worker, and all the memorable experiences—good and bad—that form the core of your relationship are present, floating between you two.

Now imagine all of the positive experiences are wires of goodwill upon which you can hang trust. All of the negative experiences are rocks of varying weights and size.

When you look at the space between you two, what are the quantity and thickness of the wires? What are the quantity and weight of the rocks? Do the wires have a fighting chance? Are there just a few pebbles, or one big gargantuan rock?

A pebble is when someone owes you five dollars and daily tells you how they mean to repay you but had to give their kid lunch money again. It's not going to break the relationship, however it's constantly in the space and you have to communicate around it. A boulder is that awful meeting two years ago when your colleague undermined you in front of your team. The trust, and thus the relationship, was broken and has not been repaired.

How do you think your co-worker sees the space between the two of you?

Stop dodging, avoiding and ignoring those rocks. Pulverize the pebbles and roll away the stones. Remember, relationships with co-workers is one of the eight critical factors to having employees feel good about coming to work.

Ever notice how easy it is to communicate with someone you're close to, "Dude, you're killing me, where's that report?" as compared to the person you're sideways with, "Mark, I know you've been really busy, I was just wondering if you could tell me when you'll have a chance to finish that report, as there's a few things I'd like to tie up?"

Now imagine the complexity of interweaving rocks and wires in a meeting of five people.

Know Conflict Styles

Before we get into "How to Communicate in Funkytown" it's good to get a read on your conflict style and that of your team. In general, we all have a "go to" conflict style when we're not our best selves. You know, those times when your nervous system takes the wheel and your mental capacity drains. Adrenaline is pumping through your veins, pupils dilate and all reasoning takes a back seat for the battle, flight or fight. When we *are* our best selves we're grounded, committed to a resolution and receptive.

Common Conflict Styles

1. **Get defensive (fight).** This looks like stepping forward, getting louder, using defensive statements, blaming others, indignation, getting blustery with large hand and arm gestures.

2. **Shut down (flight).** This is stepping back, crossing your arms, trying to melt into the wallpaper, "lights are on but no one's home" look in

your eyes, looking down, avoiding eye contact, waiting for it to be over, tuning out, closed body language, walking away, silence.

3. **Passive aggressive (combo).** In this mode, you have a snarky conversation in your head about what you would say in response, rolling your eyes, steely staring, huffing "whatever," short interjections of sarcasm, saying one thing and meaning another, under the breath comments, closed body language.

Some are consistent while others play on both ends of the spectrum depending on the relationship context—boss, peer, co-worker, direct report, family, love relationship or friends. If you're not sure what your "go-to" style is at work, just ask your co-workers. They can tell you.

As a leader, your awareness of your go-to conflict behavior gives you the option to choose a different response. If you're clueless, your style can blindside your organization.

Knowing the style of your team members is mission critical for knowing when you've lost someone in a conversation. In that moment, your communication is going through a distortion filter. Stop the conversation. Pause. Look them in the eye. And gently say, *"No one is attacking you.* I really want to figure out a solution that works for both of us." Let them take a deep breath and see if they can come back and be present. If so, regroup, starting with your intention. If not, reschedule.

If you want to take a deeper dive on conflict styles, check out Thomas Kilmann's work with five Styles—Competitive, Collaborative, Compromising, Accommodating and Avoiding.

Understand How People Get to Funkytown

"The single biggest problem in communication is the illusion that it has taken place."

—George Bernard Shaw, playwright, critic, and polemicist

Funkytown is that place where there's unspoken tension, hurt feelings, anger or confusion. The relationship is sideways. When Carly has that pit in the stomach feeling when she sees Megan, they're in Funkytown. When Mark actively avoids Jack and prays not to be put on a project with him, they're in Funkytown. If Mary awkwardly stops talking when Joe comes into the room, they're in Funkytown.

A few of the most common ways co-workers end up in Funkytown include:

- Loss of trust
- Loss of respect
- Lack of alignment
- Lack of integrity
- Lack of inclusion
- Misunderstanding
- Values prioritization
- Personality conflicts

Uncover the Source of the Relationship Breakdown

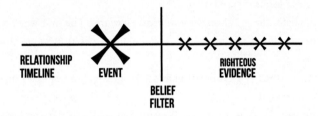

Most relationship breaks occur in a single moment or event resulting in a negative belief about the other person. We then see that person through that belief, through that filter, and continue to look for evidence to support that belief. This is so common there's even a phrase for it—confirmation bias, defined by the *Oxford English Dictionary* as "the tendency to interpret new evidence as confirmation of one's existing beliefs or theories."

I worked with a supervisor and an employee who were struggling to see eye to eye. Both were committed to the work and "good people." So it seemed baffling. What I learned was seven years earlier, after a disagreement, the employee decided the supervisor was looking to get him fired. Every word his supervisor said to him from that moment on was heard through the filter of "he's out to get me." He had been amassing proof to support his belief ever since. The supervisor had no idea. "Are you kidding me?" he said. "I have no intention of firing you. You're one of my best engineers."

Seven years of dissonance fell away in a moment.

The good news is once a break like that is resolved, the rancor and disconnect disappear quickly. Whenever I'm working on a relationship repair, one of my first questions is, "When did you realize Jane wasn't someone you could count on?" It is this moment that has to be unpacked to repair the relationship.

Assuming someone doesn't like us is another common cause of relationship breakdowns. We start treating the other person differently. Charles was positive Melissa in customer service hated his guts because she looked at him sideways on his third day. After going through the Funkytown training, he took a deep breath and reached out to her to test his assumption:

"Hey Melissa, I know this is kind of weird. But, I'm pretty sure you don't like me, and I'm not sure why."

"That's odd, because I thought you didn't like me. You avoid me like the plague," Melissa replied.

"Well that's 'cause I thought you didn't like me. The first week I was here you looked at me really odd and I was pretty sure you hated my guts."

"Mmm, I don't remember that at all. Honestly, I'm not even sure when you started."

"Wow, do I feel like a jackass. Seems like I made this all up. I'm sorry I've avoided you. That probably felt pretty crappy."

"Yeah, it did. But I'm glad to hear you don't hate me."

Relationship breakdowns brutalize productivity. According to Christine Porath and Christine Pearson's extensive research in "The Hidden Toll of Workplace Incivility" in the *McKinsey Quarterly*, when employees feel disrespected, "intentionally ignored, undermined by colleagues, or publicly belittled by an insensitive manager" the results are staggering:

- 80 percent lost work time worrying about the incident.

- 78 percent said their commitment to the organization declined.

- 66 percent said their performance declined.

- 63 percent lost work time avoiding the offender.

- 48 percent intentionally decreased their work effort.

- 47 percent intentionally decreased the time spent at work.

- 38 percent intentionally decreased the quality of their work.

- 25 percent admitted to taking their frustration out on customers.

Why We Stay in Funkytown

We stay because we hope "it" will go away. But there is only one option that will take two people out of Funkytown: a direct real-deal conversation.

The idea of having that conversation can be scary, even terrifying. Why is a direct conversation so difficult for so many people? We want to be liked and we want to belong. The fear of not being liked and not belonging is SO overwhelming it overshadows everything else.

Here are some of the reasons given for why people *actively choose* to stay in Funkytown:

- It's just not worth it.
- It's not my place or job to tell them.
- It's just easier to do myself.
- I don't like conflict.
- I don't know how she will react.
- *I know* how she will react.
- I don't want to cause problems.
- He's just a jerk.
- Nothing would change anyway.
- It'll just make the situation worse.
- I don't want to hurt his feelings.*

These reasons are commonplace and insidious. Not only do they keep you from taking a step towards the person you're struggling with, they keep confidants, friends and trusted advisers from encouraging cohorts to take that step forward towards reconciliation. Imagine your teammate comes to you complaining about Peter's unnerving inability to stay on topic. You kindly suggest she talk to Peter directly and share her concern. She then gives you one of the above reasons. *And you accept it and let her off the hook.* Because you can relate, you've used that same reason.

*This reason is the most crafty on this list because we get to look kind in our avoidance.

Caution: Sneaky Sounding Boards

I emphasize over and over how important it is to speak to someone directly. I had one man ask me, "But what if I'm talking to someone else as a sounding board?" Sounding boards are sneaky.

At their best, sounding boards help you work through a concern, consider your contribution to the situation, assess your assumptions and triggers and mold your phrasing. A genuine sounding board will insist on follow-through communication and will check in afterwards.

At their worst, sounding boards become dark corners of veiled gossip. Your sounding board understands and relates. You receive validation and do nothing because you feel better and righteous. Nothing has been resolved *and your cohort's perception of the other person has changed without that other person having an opportunity to speak to their experience or intentions.* The frustration will continue. Instead of supporting you in repairing the relationship, your sounding board has unwittingly reinforced your commitment to being liked and right.

Another possibility is that your sounding board, with the best of intentions, will offer to speak to the person you're struggling with. This doesn't work. It simply encourages cumbersome and troublesome triangulation. Intentions get misrepresented. Facts get twisted. Understanding further away.

Let's say you're the trusted advisor. You want to support your co-worker, and you don't want to gossip. What do you do? "Hey Carol, I know you're frustrated with Susie. I'd struggle with this too. You really need to talk to her directly. We're all in this department together and when the two of you don't get along, it impacts all of us. I know you two can figure it out. You're both smart, capable people with good intentions. I want what's best for you and the team. If you want to talk through how to have the conversation with her, I'm happy to help. But I don't want to talk about Susie unless you're going to reach out to her directly."

Take Four Steps Out of Funkytown

The rewards of getting out of Funkytown are enormous. Ease of work and communication is one. Liberating the daily dread of "dealing" with the other person and feeling good about coming to work is another. However the most meaningful benefit is the freedom to be the person you believe yourself to be.

My friend told me she knew the day when she *had* to talk directly to her co-worker, Bill. She found herself headed to the break room with her coffee cup and upon seeing Bill, averted her gaze and tried to head back to her desk unnoticed. He asked, "How was your weekend Pam?" In her head, she sneered, "I don't know BILL, how was *your* weekend?" She was horrified by her own inner voice—who was this lady? Here she was snide, cynical and insincere—even if only in her own head. She believed herself to be someone who was kind, generous and open-minded. That person would have the courage to talk to Bill directly.

So how do you get from here to there? Take these four key steps.

One—Self Reflection

Evaluate why this individual hits a nerve. Take some time to cull through your annoyed mind—your thoughts, behaviors, past experiences, insecurities and fears. What is triggering you? Where are you hooked? Does this experience bring to light something you would prefer hidden? Are you embarrassed about how you handled the situation? Are you the common denominator in similar experiences with others in your life? Keep digging until you reach the insight that makes sense.

Let go of the anger. If your intention is to get something off your chest, you've already lost. If you come from a place of anger, your co-worker will run to the safety of their conflict style. This could look like mirroring your aggression or getting quiet and nodding in response, neither of which is productive. It makes the conversation all about you and your anger and reduces your co-worker's ability to take responsibility for his role in the situation. It becomes about how you're a jerk.

Anger is an easier form of expression than fear or hurt. Fear and hurt require vulnerability. Vulnerability is foundational for a real deal conversation. To uncover vulnerability, ask, "How do I feel?" Then ask a few more times. The deeper you go, the easier it is for the other person to relate. Perhaps you feel embarrassed, ignored, shocked, ashamed, stupid, confused, disappointed or disrespected. These are all feelings we've painfully held at one point or another. Instead of feeling attacked, your co-worker can feel empathy.

Let go of assumptions. We get in trouble when we create meaning to fill a void of information. Ask, what are the facts of the situation—*as you understand them?* Know there's a good chance you're missing a piece of information. What are you confused about? Also, did you make an assumption or fabricate meaning?

For example, John didn't invite you to the meeting. To you, this meant he doesn't want your input. The only fact is, to your knowledge, John didn't invite you to the meeting. Your confusion is about why. Perhaps you missed his email, perhaps the meeting was rescheduled, perhaps he was trying to save you time. Who knows? Not you, yet.

Shortcuts after Self-Reflection

Clean it up. If you already know you're the source of the problem, own it. You're not the first person who defended and deflected when some-one pointed out your error. Apologize for the impact you had on the other person—the sooner the better. As a friend of mine says, "It's easier to eat crow when it's hot, 'cause it will darn near kill ya when it goes down cold and congealed."

If you think it's all in your head, ask. If you think you're making an assumption, go to the other person and ask, "Is there any truth in this?"

Two—Mentally Prepare How You Will Show Up

Be clear about your intentions and imagine your ideal outcome. Ideally, you want to share your perspective, and understand the other person's perspective, about why things went sideways and then together figure out how to repair the relationship. If your intentions are not noble, do not have the conversation. An ideal outcome may be as simple as having a good working relationship with this person.

Let go of assumptions about what will happen. How many times have you had an argument with another person BEFORE you've even started talking to them? You did a fantastic job of playing both parts of the conversation and have it all figured out how it's going to go. We all do this. Ultimately you don't know how this person will react. If you're thinking, I've tried to talk to this person before and they're always defensive, chances are you tried once and didn't follow these steps. Be open to the possibility this will be a positive exchange. Your ideal outcome is, after all, possible.

Come from a place of genuine curiosity. Start in humble wonderment rather than knowing judgment. The phrases "can you help me understand" or "I was curious why" are powerful especially when facts follow. For example, "John, I noticed you had a meeting the other day about the project and I'm curious why I wasn't included?" versus "John, why didn't you want my input on the project?"

Your tone is important. You can ask through gritted teeth and furrowed brow, or with an open face expressing a true desire to understand. Remember when your mother would shriek, "What were *you* thinking!!?" as compared to when your bushy-browed grandfather slowly tapped his glasses against his teeth and with a quizzical look inquired, "Tell me, what *were* you thinking?"

Trust the other person's intentions. Most people in their heart of hearts are good. They don't intend harm. They try to do the best they can with the information and skills they have. Bad behavior does occur, and when it does, 95 percent of the time the core motivator is fear, shame or a desire to prove oneself. So understand where bad behavior begins. Be compassionate. Rarely does a person wake up and think, "I want to be a crappy co-worker today."

Identify common ground and be a stand. Instead of focusing on differences, look for common ground. What do you both care about? Family? Kids? Your city? The mission of the organization? Trying to make a living? Be a stand for what you both care about that's more far-reaching than the spat between you two. "We both care about this place and want to see it succeed." "We both care about this team." "We both have families we're trying to support." "We're both trying to do the best we can do." Launch from common ground and use these words as the first step to building a better working relationship together.

When You Don't Trust Their Intentions...

Now if you really don't trust someone's intentions, if you feel they are genuinely out to sabotage or undermine you, this will be key to first communicate in the fourth step. Make sure you have specific examples to explain why you feel the way you do. "I find it difficult to believe what you say to me in private when you act differently in public. I've noticed this a few times, like when.... Am I mistaken?" Or "I wish I could trust your intentions. But as crazy as this sounds, I literally feel like you'd like to see me fired. My sense of this is because.... Am I totally off-base?"

Three—Invite Them to the Conversation

Here's where the rubber meets the road. Until now, it's been all you, self-reflecting and mentally preparing. This is the shortest and hardest step. Whenever you invite someone to a conversation there is a possibility your invitation will be declined. Yet this is where the real-deal magic begins. Without this step, all your preparation is wasted.

You want your invitation to be simple, short and relaxed.

Follow these five steps:

1. Say exactly and simply what's amiss.

2. Express humility.*

3. Express your intentions.

4. Ask for their participation.

5. Define a good time to meet face to face.

*You must include humility for the invitation to work. Expressing humility creates a critical opening in the conversation for new awareness and thus a new outcome. Humility admits to the possibility your assumptions may be inaccurate. Humility also consists of owning your role. This vulnerability allows the other person to reflect, acknowledge and be honest about their own assumptions and role.

I've found this paradigm is best understood in examples. Here are several:

Recent event—"Hey John, ever since our exchange in that meeting the other day, I've felt a tension between the two of us.(1) Maybe I'm off-base,(2) but I'd love to get it cleared up because I want to have a good working relationship with you.(3) Would you be willing to touch base this Friday at 10?(4, 5)

Long held grudge—"Hey Tom, for whatever reason you and I have never gotten along well.(1) We work together every day. It's crazy we've let it go on this long. I know it stresses me out, and I know I haven't been exactly warm and fuzzy.(2) I wish we had a decent working relationship.(3) Would you be willing to meet this Friday to see if we can figure out how to get from here to there?"(4, 5)

Accountability—"Hey Carol, two weeks ago you said you would have the report completed. I haven't seen it.(1) I know I'm not always super organized, so maybe I'm missing something here.(2) As colleagues, I want to know we're on the same page.(3) Would you be willing to touch base this afternoon to get this figured out?"(4, 5)

Consider writing a draft of your invitation so it rolls off your tongue more casually.

Here's what NOT to do in your invitation:

- Say, "We need to meet," "We need to talk," or "I've got a bone to pick with you."

- Try to be funny. You want to demonstrate sincere interest and not confuse your invitee regarding your intentions.

- Couch your communication. Couched communication causes confusion. Instead say exactly and simply what is amiss.

- Get into the weeds of the situation. When you invite the other person, they may ask you to have the conversation on the spot. Don't accept. It's important the other person has time to process beforehand. Remember, your invitee hasn't done self-reflection or mental preparation yet. If their conflict style is defensive, they may assert, "Well why don't we talk about it right now!?" When they ask for an on the spot meeting, they are nervous and want to get it over with as soon as possible. You can simply say, "While I appreciate your desire to talk now, I'd really prefer we wait until Friday. This meeting is important to our relationship and I want it to be thoughtful rather than impromptu."

Once a day and time have been set for the conversation, you are on your way.

Congratulations, the time to leave Funkytown is close at hand.

What happens if someone doesn't accept your invitation? While rare, this could happen. Stay grounded. Stay committed. There is a good chance it's their conflict style speaking. Respond, "Know my invitation stands. I really would like to have a good working relationship with you. Whenever you're ready to talk, I'll be here." A few weeks later they'll likely ask you to go grab lunch.

Four—Have the Conversation

The majority of the conversation is giving voice to what you uncovered in steps one and two. Review your mental preparation before the meeting. Lead the meeting since you provided the invitation. Set the tone. Speak slowly and thoughtfully. Keep your intention to understand and to learn at the forefront. Look them in the eye and open the conversation:

Acknowledge common ground. Name what you both care about that's more important than your discord. At least acknowledge you're both trying to do the best you can.

Restate your intentions. Repeat the one you stated in your invitation. Consistency is comforting.

Restate what is. Repeat exactly and simply what's amiss.

Define, as you understand it, the facts of what happened. And ask, "Is that accurate? Am I missing a piece?"

Speak to the impact the discord has had on you. Unless you are a manager, do not speak about the impact on the team or others. This implies gossip and can take a dark turn.

Own your part in the situation. Speak to your role.

Reveal assumptions. In an ideal world, you wouldn't have any. But the reality is you do. Speak to them. Ask, "Are these assumptions correct? Or am I off-base?"

Express vulnerability. Vulnerability is particularly powerful for an open conversation. It shows a genuine commitment to the conversation. It also softens the space and makes it safe to share genuine feelings.

Phrases to consider:

- I'm really confused. How did we get here?

- I'm nervous to have this conversation because I'm afraid it'll just make things worse.

- You said you would do X and I see Y. Can you help me understand the disconnect?

- You're really important to me and the way this is going down feels crappy and I don't know how to turn it around.

- I feel like an idiot. Can you help me understand...?

- Can you help me understand why you're so frustrated with me?

- I know something's not right, but I simply can't see it. What am I missing?

- I literally stayed up last night worried about...

Listen for understanding. Listen like there is no one else in the world and nowhere else in the world you'd rather be. You're that committed. Don't interrupt. Take notes. I cannot emphasize enough the power of having someone truly feeling heard.

Stay steady. The other person may get defensive. The conversation may turn heated. They may have been preparing for battle while you were preparing for peace. Continue to wave the white flag until they can see it. Continue to be a stand for the relationship. "Mary, I understand why you might have thought I didn't want your input. But honestly, I thought you had a finish line that day and I didn't want to interrupt you for what I considered a relatively insignificant project meeting. I'm sorry you felt excluded. I'm very interested in your input on this project."

Consider solutions together and make requests. Talk about how you two can make sure this doesn't happen again. How can you avoid the pitfalls that got you here? What do each of you need to do moving forward? Finally, discuss behavior that needs to change. "I would like to ask, next time will you please come talk to me directly?"

Here are examples of what this could sound like all together:

"Monica we've been working here for a few years. I know you care about this client as much as I do. As I mentioned the other day, I really would like us to be a united front. Since the beginning of this last phase it's felt like we aren't aligned. I think we got sideways when I went to Joanna instead of coming to you about leading the project. Is this your sense? I know you're usually the project manager. I assumed you wouldn't have given me the opportunity to lead since this project is your baby. Is this true? I've felt your cold shoulder. We used to work so well together. Looking back I wish I would've asked you first. I'm at a loss as far as where to go from here, but I really wanted to see what we could do to repair this relationship. What are your thoughts?

"Carl we're both committed to solving this problem. My hope is we can solve it together. Unfortunately, from my perspective, in the last few weeks it feels like our efforts have become competitive rather than collaborative. Is this your experience too? I've missed our brainstorming magic and riffing off of one another's ideas. I tend to be competitive by nature and so I've been wondering if I'm the one who created this disconnect. I would suggest it doesn't help that we're both up for the same promotion. Is there something else I'm missing? I'd love to figure out how we can get back to having one another's backs and finding the best solution together. What are your thoughts?

I had one person in this training ask, "I don't want to screw up, is it okay if I write down and read my talking points?" Absolutely, and you can even tell the other person, "This conversation is really important to me and I didn't want to screw it up, so I wrote down some talking points. I hope you don't mind if I lean on them." If nothing else, they will think you were thoughtful in your preparation. They'll be able to relate to your nervousness and appreciate your desire to have this go well.

Invariably someone asks, **"What if the person I'm in Funkytown with is my boss?"** Here's what I want you to remember: like all of us, bosses are simply fallible human beings unaware of their own blind spots. Just like you would for a co-worker, be a stand for their success. It just requires a bit more courage on your part.

Unfortunately few leaders get this type of direct feedback because of employee's fear of authority. Because leadership plays such a critical role and has such a large impact, they need to hear from you. If you're kind, candid and constructive, if you show up with humility and curiosity, a true leader will welcome your input, and your bravery. As occurred with one of my courageous executive clients, you may be surprised to find yourself as one of the CEO's trusted advisors.

In my experience, most of these conversations result in a deeper understanding of one another's perspective. Sometimes the outcome is alignment or an apology. Sometimes it's agreeing to disagree. Other times it's a slap-your-forehead realization of the misunderstanding that caused the disconnect.

However in those very rare instances where it all goes to hell in a hand basket (I honestly haven't heard of this happening yet following these steps), you're never worse off for having the conversation.

Here's why. Think about all the time and energy you've spent brooding, venting, strategizing and possibly obsessing over this discord. Think of this quote:

> "Promise me you will not spend so much time treading water and trying to keep your head above the waves that you forget, truly forget, how much you have always loved to swim."
>
> **Tyler Knott Gregson,** poet and photographer

What you're up to in the world is bigger than this discord. Your time, mind space and energy is spent better elsewhere. By choosing to have this conversation, even if it goes awry, means you get to swim. You can let go knowing you tried. You chose to be the person you believe yourself to be.

Conflict Resolution Between Two Key Employees

You have two employees who can't stand each other. They're beyond unkind. Everyone on the team knows it. He can't stand her. She despises him. The rest of the team watches, cringing at potential landmines. The drama is draining. All it takes is two employees to wreak havoc and distract from the work at hand. You want to fire both of them and be done already. The only thing holding you back is they're both significant contributors. But you're also aware of the expensive inefficiency and disruption they cause the rest of the team. Everyone is wondering why you haven't addressed the situation.

What are you to do when two employees who have been valuable assets to the organization are now liabilities?

First, avoid these pitfalls:

- Give a stern lecture with knit eyebrows about how they have to get along. This addresses the issue, but doesn't resolve it. It could also be perceived as condescending. Regardless, often both will behave for a period of time to get off the hot seat and then they'll be back at it.

- Send a memo reminding everyone of the importance of teamwork.

- Hope the issue will eventually go away, allowing for the fighting to reach a blowout.

- Rashly fire both employees, lose two key contributors and feel the long-lasting repercussions from the remaining employees' compassion to their plight.

Instead, meet with each person individually. Do not mince words. Be clear about the impact their infighting has on their co-workers, your customers and the organization's reputation. Ultimately they are undermining the mission. This continued interaction is no longer an option. In fact, you regret having allowed it for this long. You value each one's contribution to the organization and you're willing to give it one last effort, IF and ONLY IF, each one of them is committed to a resolution and willing to have the tough conversations to get there. Ask them both to go home, sleep on it and return in a couple of days with either a letter of resignation or a commitment to working towards a successful working relationship.

If one of them gets belligerent and launches into how it's the other person's fault, and how maybe they need to find another job, let them.

If both express interest in reconciliation, then individually ask them the questions below and let them know you will be meeting with them together to resolve old grudges and address areas of misunderstanding and avoid triggers:

- How do you feel about the other person?

- How do you think the other person feels about you? Why do you think this and what do you know to be fact?

- When was the first time you realized this person was someone you struggle to get along with?

- What does the other person do or say that really bothers you? What triggers you?

- What do you think you do or say that frustrates the other person?

- Do you trust the other person wants what's best for the team and the organization?
- Do you think the other person trusts you want what's best for the team and the organization?
- What do you appreciate about the other person?
- What is your role in this situation? How have you contributed?
- Do you owe the other person an apology?
- What could you do to improve this relationship?

Now look at the information you garnered from each individual. What do you see? Where are the REAL pitfalls in the relationship, the source not just the symptoms? What dynamics are at play? What is the genuine hurt behind the stories?

Now, think about how you are going to bring these insights to the table. As the facilitator, your language is key. Choose language that accurately reflects what was said and allows for consideration and conversation.

For instance, Carly tells you, "Everyone knows Michael isn't reliable, he can't be counted on and I'm always cleaning up his messes" (and provides several legitimate examples). Carly also shares she hasn't spoken to Michael directly about these instances.

When you bring them together, the conversation might start like this: "Michael, Carly struggles with knowing she can count on you. Sometimes it's work tasks such as calling a client when you said you would. Sometimes it's following agreed-upon processes like receiving the purchase order before having the team begin the work. Carly acknowledges that in all fairness you haven't had a chance to address these since she hasn't been forthright about her concerns."

In the meeting, make sure not to back down. Be brave and bring up the contentious topics. These have to be addressed. Don't let them wiggle out of it. If you can tell someone is acquiescing or placating, call them on it. Let them know you are truly committed to the success of their relationship. To continue being a valuable part of the team, they have to resolve these issues.

 Favorite Resource: One of my all-time favorite resources for learning more about kind, candid and constructive communication is *Conscious Business* by Fred Kofman.

Funkytown is a tough place to visit, let alone live. Relationship break-downs are damaging for the team and devastating for the organization. Left unchecked, those elephants will destroy every last bit of culture. Don't delay. Bear hug conflict.

Chapter 10

Create Culture
Conducive to Change

- Embrace These Eight Key Change Steps
- Speak to the Heart and the Mind Will Follow
- Talk through Change
- Implement Successful Change

| Supervisor | Meaning/ Job Fit | Impact | Organizational Support | Organizational Fit |

"Are you green and growing or ripe and rotting?"

—Ray Kroc, McDonald's mogul

Is your team stuck in analysis paralysis? Do team members groan every time you suggest a new initiative? Do they nod, do nothing, and hope to wait you out?

People fear the unknown change brings. Like a barnacle stuck to a sinking ship, they proclaim, "I may not be going anywhere, but at least I know my place." The known cuddles comfort. Studies show teams prefer a consistently horrible boss over one who's unpredictable. One team I worked with texted as they came into the office, "What's the weather?" to get a read on their moody manager. They wanted to prepare and adjust accordingly. People find security in both knowing what to expect and the expected.

In addition to habit and comfort, another obstacle often overlooked when making strategic changes is that we are creatures of our own competency. No one likes feeling stupid. Change is uncomfortable and can feel dismissive, especially when someone has earned their stripes and is considered one of the go-to experts. Feeling as clueless as a new employee can feel like a betrayal. They were *the* inner circle. Now they're on the outside like everyone else. Overnight there's a loss of value, credibility and identity. Here change equals loss, a personal loss.

Studies about loss aversion show we hate losing more than we love winning, even if our odds of winning are twice as favorable. Loss is scary. **So how do you create a culture conducive to change when people don't want to lose their place?** How do you create an attitude of "If we don't play, we can't win?" How do you encourage your team to risk trying something new and see it as an opportunity to move your organization closer to success?

Embrace These Eight Key Change Steps

1. **Communicate: if we don't play, if we don't consistently innovate, we will lose.** Share the sad stories of Blockbuster and Kodak who didn't play in the world of online streaming media and digital photography. They lost. Think of Facebook who moved beyond the comfort of colleges. It won. Think of Google which played beyond the role of search engine with Adwords. They won. Yahoo wallflowered.

    To play is to change. To change is to play. Try, learn, adjust. Know the three kinds of change:

    A. **Chosen Change** is change we choose and try to control. Think of life choices such as moving, marriage, or leaving for a different job. Consider work choices such as marketing strategy, team make-up or product innovation.

B. **Forced Uncontrolled Change** is change we didn't choose. It chooses us and we cannot control it. Think of life events like storms, accidents or illnesses. Consider work events like a key vendor closing, regulatory changes or market shifts in the cost of commodities.

C. **Forced Controlled Change** is change we didn't choose and often can't control, but is controlled by others. In this category are politics, road construction and the new neighbor's barking dog. In the workplace consider competitor price cutting, dress code and mandatory meetings.

This last kind of change most upsets our sense of self-determination. We want to have more of a say in the matter. We bristle when things are decided for us, even if at times we would have chosen the same option.

2. **Tell your team you wish all change could be chosen, known and controllable.** Promise you will do your best to keep them apprised of upcoming changes. When possible you will seek and consider their input prior to taking action. However, also mention change is often unpredictable and in moments of chaos and crisis you need to be decisive and their aligned action is critical.

3. **Leadership cannot serve flavor of the month.** Change has to be in alignment with the focused vision. Otherwise it's just "Squirrel!" Your team has to know changes have been thoughtfully evaluated. They have to know there is a method to the madness; that their efforts to shift towards a new "way" won't be squandered. It cannot feel like someone just came back from an industry conference and jumped on the latest untested idea.

4. **Speak to why change is positive even when outcomes are unknown.** Change challenges us to expand our comfort zone. Butterflies keep us on our toes. We gain opportunities to learn and uncover valuable insights. Career development at its best. Change makes serendipity and magic possible.

"The work I did is the work I know, and the work I do is the work I don't know. That's why I can't tell you, I don't know what I'm doing. And it's the not knowing that makes it interesting."

—**Philip Glass**, music composer

5. **Address the reality of change.** It's not perfect. Sometimes it looks like two stumbles forward, one step to the side and one step back. The team may need to try things on and see if they fit. When they don't, it's a great example of failing forward. Tell stories about changes in the past that were successful, and speak about ones that weren't and what you learned as a result. With particularly difficult changes, make sure you speak to the discomfort. Don't soft sell it.

6. **Underscore the humor and humanity of change.** Emphasize that you're all going through this together. Change is a journey. Acknowledge that sometimes change is just messy. Ask your team to keep their sense of humor. Stress that while they can't always control change, they can always control their response, attitude, words and actions.

7. **Share Stanford University Psychologist Carol Dweck's insightful paradigm** of the Growth Mindset vs. Fixed Mindset from her book *Mindset: The New Psychology of Success.*

 Favorite Resource: Carol Dweck outlines in *Mindset: The New Psychology of Success* how to be more focused on learning rather than looking good. I recommend this book to all of the perfectionists and naysayers out there. Also consider checking out John Kotter's extensive work on leading change.

8. **Lastly, answer "What's in it for me?"** Share how the change benefits their workplace experience. Perhaps they get to expand their contribution to the mission. Or it will create more ease, money and time in the long-term. Maybe it simply increases pride in being part of an organization who is innovative rather than status quo.

Speak to the Heart and the Mind Will Follow

If our hearts believe it, our minds will justify it.

The heart chooses our truth. Our hearts can talk ourselves into and out of just about anything. We will find, sometimes even create, the needed evidence to support our beliefs.

When we listen to our hearts, there is little contemplation. "It just feels right." "I know in my heart of hearts." The heart sparks movement and creates momentum. So often we speak to the mind, and the heart raises an eyebrow. Is she moved? Does she care? We try to convince with reasonable reasons and sensible sense.

The next time you're looking to get your team "on board," garner "buy in," or have success in change management, ask yourself, what would I say if I was speaking to their hearts?

I had a healthcare client who wanted to overhaul the company's core operating software. He was frustrated. He told his team, "We're excited that one of our goals for 2017 is to update our old operating system." His announcement was met with sighs and groans. Seeing the response, he proceeded with his PowerPoint of stats that proved the value of the new system. They were still less than enthused. While they understood the rationale behind the new software, all they could see was the heavy lifting and annoying frustrations of learning a new system.

I recommended he speak to their hearts.

At their next all-hands meeting, he tried again. "Last time I announced our goal to overhaul our software. Will this be hard? Yep. Will this be frustrating? Most definitely. And what challenge worth taking on isn't? This is a mountain we have to move to advance our mission of "Giving Life." By December 31st of this year, we'll be able to respond to our clients twice as fast and reduce inefficiencies by half. We'll reduce mistakes and time wasting errors. This means we can more than double our impact! DOUBLE. We can give twice as much life!"

His enthusiasm was beginning to spread.

"Your time and energy will be better spent in doing what you came here to do. Every day your efforts will go twice as far. So yes, will this transformation be uncomfortable? No doubt. And I believe this team will go the distance. As we trip and stumble we'll get back up again knowing we're one step closer. Thank you for caring and thank you for bringing your A game and making this company the best it can be. Together we are unstoppable!"

As a leader, motivational speaking is a key tool in your toolbox. Speak to their hearts and watch their minds follow.

Action Jackson:
Talk through Change

First talk with your team about how they experience change:

● In general, are you someone who likes change or can't stand it?
  Why?

● What changes have you enjoyed at our organization?

● What changes have been frustrating, hard or scary?

Talk with your team about how they can support change:

● If there's ambiguity and you need clarity, get it.

● If you're concerned, express it constructively.

● Don't be attached to the way things used to be.

● Celebrate being uncomfortable—you're learning.

● Learn from and lean on each other.

● Trust the intentions of one another and the organization.

● Expect it won't go perfectly and have empathy.

Then have your team discuss with one another:

● Do you have any concerns about future changes?

● What is the top thing you hope never changes at our organization?

● If there was only one thing you could change about our organization, what would it be? (Note, before you ask this question, be
  committed to taking concrete action on one or two meaningful
  insights from the feedback.)

● What is the one thing you can do tomorrow to help support change
  at our organization?

Action Jackson:
Implement Successful Change

Next time you want to launch a new initiative or alter a current process, consider the following:

1. Choose your changes wisely. Does it meet the criteria of your mission, vision and values? Knowing it will require resources shifted from other priorities, is this change more important than what you've already committed to? As an organization, if we say yes to this, what are we saying no to? Triple check it's not a "flavor of the month."

2. If successful, what will this change do for the organization? If unsuccessful, what will be learned? What could be lost? How much of a risk is this *really*?

3. Be cognizant of timing. Is there value in waiting to incorporate this into the next set of strategic goals or does it need to be implemented now? Why? Is this really the best time? Will there ever be a good time?

4. What's the implementation plan? How will you measure progress? What are the milestones? Who's championing this effort? Who needs to be involved?

5. Do we have the infrastructure and resources to support this effort?

6. If possible, BEFORE YOU LAUNCH, take a few days. During that time, share with your team what you're thinking of implementing and ask for their input.

Share:

- Why this change is important.

- What this change could do for the organization.

- The options that were considered.

- Why you think this is the best option.

- Why now.

- Based on what you know, the best case and worst case scenario.

- The proposed implementation plan.

Then listen, intently. Take notes. Don't respond to concerns brought forth in the moment. Just listen and capture.

Ask if anything else occurs to them in the next 48 hours to please let you know.

Then sleep on it. Review and assess their concerns. Are they valid? Have you addressed them? Should this be a pilot initiative instead?

Send out a communication shortly after, detailing answers to their concerns. Communicate clearly if the project is green-lighted or is on temporary hold to evaluate and address concerns brought to the table.

. . . .

So, are you and your team green and growing? Overcome loss aversion. Be thoughtful when implementing change and make sure to acknowledge change is hard. Speak to their hearts and encourage boldness along with adventurous confidence. Then watch as your team nimbly changes course as needed and rallies through unexpected challenges.

Chapter 11

Expand Time
and Boost Focus

- Honor 2000 Hours

- Shift Your Relationship with Time

- Put Strategic Work on the Front Burner

- Decide What to Delegate

Supervisor

Co-workers

Impact

**Work-Family
Climate**

"Tiiiiiiiiime, is on my side, yes it is."

–The Rolling Stones

Your time is now. Lead with urgency. Drive purpose and progress. However, be thoughtful to avoid paralyzing panic and obstructing overwhelm. This chapter will help you walk this tight rope.

Honor 2,000 Hours

Work and life are not something to balance. There is no work-life "balance." They are not separate.

Work takes place inside life. Work is a part of life.

On average we spend 2,000 hours a year working. 2,000 hours of human contribution. That's 2,000 out of 5,840 waking hours spent contributing and creating the success of your organization. That's 2,000 hours of *your* life. Of *your* blood, sweat and tears. All of your circumstances, experiences and choices, brought you to this place, to this time, to work with this team.

We all have 24 hours in a day and seven days a week. We hope we have enough time to do our life's work and to fulfill our life's purpose. Every year, every individual on your team gives you 2,000 hours of their blood, sweat and tears. Make their contribution worth it.

> "Of all wastes, the greatest waste that you can commit is the waste of labour... You perhaps think, 'to waste the labour of men is not to kill them.' Is it not? I should like to know how you could kill them more utterly."
>
> **—John Ruskin,** author of *The Crown of Wild Olive*, 1866.

There is no time to waste. There is no life to waste.

Shift Your Relationship with Time

Time isn't concrete. It can fly or drag. We know what it feels like to be "in the zone" where hours fly by *and* we feel accomplished. Time feels rich when we have an insight, experience forward progress, accomplish a challenging task, connect meaningfully with another or generate thoughtful breathing space. We also know what it feels like to be on hold with the insurance company, listening to Muzak, desperate for a simple answer. It's when time feels like sand slipping through your fingers that overwhelm occurs. Time wasted is opportunity lost.

Are these refrains common in your language, or that of your team?

- "I don't have enough time."
- "I have a zillion things to do."
- "I'm swamped."
- "So much to do, so little time."
- "I never get anything done."

If so, you have a problem. An extraordinary workplace culture does not thrive when overwhelmed. Anxiety, dread, despair, paralysis, and procrastination flourish instead.

Remember, your team is a reflection of you. If phrases like these often fly out of your mouth with the greatest of ease, don't be surprised if they become team mantras as well as team scapegoats.

You are not a victim of time. Time is the one equalizer. We all have 168 hours a week. We all choose how we spend our time. Yet we have a socially acceptable epidemic in using "busyness" as a scapegoat for not living lives we love.

I often wrestle with this alligator. Every few months, when my mindset relapses, I have to remind myself to stop pretending I'm a victim of time. I have to look honestly at my choices. For example, it's not true I don't have enough time to exercise. What is true is I choose to spend time with my family instead of exercising. Or watch Netflix. Or write this book. In those moments, I have to acknowledge I'm not choosing health. Instead I'm choosing connection, relaxation or a sense of accomplishment. While all three of these are also important to me, I have to decide my health comes first. Then I go get my sweat on. Kris one, alligator zero.

Change the way time is perceived and experienced.

Time demands respect. Like money, time needs to be budgeted. Unlike money, you can't make more time. Once it has passed, it is gone forever.

The definition of time in the *Shorter Oxford English Dictionary* fills more than a page of that tiny type. How do you define time?

There's clock time and real time. We live in real time where time flies when you're enjoying yourself or drags when you're not. Real time is mental. It is your creation. Anything you create, you can manage. There are no limitations. You can **give yourself more time**, more breathing room. I often ran minutes late. Stressed, I would speed into the parking lot, screech to a stop, scramble to grab my purse, and run into a meeting. The duress increasingly became a problem. So I began to give myself 10 extra minutes of drive time before each appointment. This made me a safer driver, reduced my daily deadly stress cortisol, allowed me to not disappoint myself and demonstrated respect for the person I was meeting. I also gave myself 15 minutes in the morning. Instead of setting my alarm for the time I wanted to wake up, and then hitting snooze for 15 minutes and starting my day off eating dust, I set the alarm for 15 minutes before I want to wake up and then again for the time I need to wake up.

Change your language about time. Don't say, "There's never enough hours in the day!" Try: "Between work, my kids' soccer, time with my beloved, rock climbing and painting the house, my life is really full. The truth is I choose it all. I wouldn't have it any other way." Instead of grumbling about the number of tasks on your plate, examine the purpose for each task and why it is important. If it's not, drop it to the bottom of the list or remove it.

Be aware of how you frame things. Call due dates finish lines instead of deadlines. Your team would rather feel like they're crossing a finish line, victory arms in the air, than a deadline, a word born of the boundary line that if crossed by a prisoner meant he would be shot dead.

Manage your mood. Remember, emotions are contagious. Let's say you toss and turn all night, you wake to the stench of your dog's vomit, your bagel lands cream cheese side down and traffic is maddening. You arrive at the office in a foul mood. Next time your day starts that poorly, consider putting on your favorite song and car dancing on the way to work. I guarantee your mood will shift.

There's much we can't control. However, we can control our beliefs, our thoughts, our attitude, our words, our actions and our behaviors. We can choose how we show up. I used to be a "hangry" person. When my blood sugar plummeted, so did my mood. My lack of consideration has now been replaced by a stash of almonds.

Fill your energy bucket. More energy gives you more rich time. Invest in your energy. Sleep, eat well, exercise. Take mental breaks. Do what brings you joy. Create and follow morning, afternoon and evening rituals that support your vitality. Know your peak productivity time.

Choose progress over perfectionism. We've all been there, paralyzed by minutiae. Attention to too much detail, fearful of not looking good. Ask, does it matter? To whom? Three years from now, will it matter? I appreciate excellence, but I appreciate darn good progress more.

Stay present to slow down time. In the *Art of Noticing*, Ellen Langer recommends actively noticing new things daily. What do you notice that's new about your workplace experience? Someone brought in a new kind of coffee. Bob got a new pair of blue suede shoes. That flickering overhead light finally got fixed.

Audit your time. For one week, write down how you spend your time in 30-minute blocks. Notice...

- What do you spend time on?
- Where is your time well spent? What are "time sucks?"
- When are you the most productive? Least productive?
- What are the circumstances that help you be your most productive?
- When is your down time?
- When do you procrastinate? Why?

Break down your time. Budget your calendar to figure out how you're going to spend your time for the week. Often we operate in hour-long chunks of time. But strategic bite-size tasks such as a phone call, initial research, or a check-in meeting with a co-worker can usually be accomplished in 20-minute blocks. Conversations and meetings expand to take the time allotted. Allot less.

Choose bite-size strategic steps. When you're in overwhelm with "everything" you have to do, my friend recommends the fog effect, where all you can see, and all you can you do, is the thing right in front of you. You can only accomplish one thing at a time. Everything else is outside of your periphery. Those things are not important now.

Narrow your focus. Part of what creates a sense of accomplishing something is accomplishing something. You can't make progress if you're not clear what you're working on. Every afternoon before you leave work, ask what's the one thing you could do that would strategically and meaningfully move the ball forward tomorrow? Write down your top one to three tasks to accomplish the next day on a post-it note (keep this separate from your long-term laundry to-do list). Then protect your productivity time to accomplish them.

Two tools you can purchase online to help narrow your personal focus: the three month SELF Journal which aligns intention with action and Focus@will which provides music that neurologically helps you focus.

Protect your plate. If someone is asking you to add something to your plate and it's full, have a conversation about priorities. Clarify, what would you like me to take off to make room for this new item? Often, this conversation will be with yourself.

Close your open door policy. If you're like most, constant interruptions drive you crazy. As the leader, it's ideal you have your sanity, as well as time to think and act strategically. You can't afford to constantly be interrupted. Yet the intention behind an open door policy to encourage openness and transparency is still a good one. How do you achieve both?

Hold office hours. Pick a consistent time that works for you and your team to touch base daily. Define what constitutes an appropriate interruption outside of those hours. Then hold them sacred and be present.

Employees often tell me, "My boss is good people, but I hate it when she says her door is open and we should come to her with our concerns. Her door is physically open, but whenever I go to talk to her, I don't think she really hears me. She stays looking at her computer, typing and nods occasionally. Or if I catch her away from her office she's constantly on her cell phone. It just makes me feel invisible, like why bother."

Trust me, I get it. You're running a mile a minute trying to get it all done. But you can't simultaneously tell people you care and then not mentally show up.

If you need to finish a thought, an e-mail or a project, just ask your team member to give you five minutes or two hours until you can give them your full attention. Set your timer if need be. Before meeting with them, take a deep breath, get into your body, feel your feet on the floor, and listen as if there was no one else in the world and nowhere else you have to be.

One CEO has met this challenge with flying colors. He has both a daily pulse on his entire company and time to focus on strategic activities. Instead of having his employees come to him, he goes to his employees. Every morning he does walk-around meetings of 15–20 minutes for each of his six departments. In each of those departments there is a communication board. On that communication board are the items to be reviewed in the daily meeting:

- Current Projects
- Key Performance Metrics (Hitting? If not hitting, why?)
- New Ideas (to review, discuss and decide)

Almost every issue that arises during the day can wait until the following morning and goes up on the communication board. If it truly can't wait a day, employees seek him out.

Put Strategic Work on the Front Burner

Strategic work is intimidating and challenging. It taxes your creative powers. Navigating the unknown and testing new ground requires vulnerability because you might get it wrong. Another challenge to strategic work is that gratification is often delayed and the work may be tedious and not terribly heroic.

This is why strategic work is often put on the backburner. Procrastination reigns as we embrace the dopamine hit of checking off easy items on the to-do list. Do you belong to the club of productive procrastinators? You may also be the type who, as you push aside strategic work, jumps in to help save the day, enjoying the immediate rush of validation.

But here's the kicker, strategic work is incredibly rewarding. When accomplished, it creates powerful momentum. There's a deep sense of profound progress.

Remember Lucille Ball and Ethel Mertz in the chocolate factory? When the conveyor belt starts screaming by, they scramble to stuff the chocolates into their mouths, down their shirts and in their hats. If you ran in to help them shove more chocolates into more crannies, you would be praised on the spot. It feels good in the moment, though tomorrow, the chocolates will continue to fly and everyone will continue spinning their wheels. Insert exasperation and frustration due to wasted time here. However the strategic less glamorous work to be done is to take on figuring out how to fix the conveyor belt.

> *Do the work of the work. Make progress. Feel accomplished. Repeat.*

Smile. You're bringing joy to the workplace.

 Action Jackson:
Decide What to Delegate

Grab a white board or piece of flip chart paper and try this simple exercise:

1. Write down a laundry list of everything you do and everything you're responsible for in a given month.

2. Circle in green everything you enjoy and that gives you energy.

3. Circle in orange everything you're really good at.

4. Circle in blue everything that's strategic, that will move your organization forward.

5. Circle in red everything ONLY YOU can do. Push yourself to answer this one strictly, meaning if you were out of the country or got hit by a bus could someone else do it?

6. Now take it in. What do you notice?

7. Some items might be circled multiple times. Keep these.

8. Some items have no circles. Delegate these items. Find someone who has this skill or train someone. Keep in mind this is a great opportunity for growth for the person you entrust.

9. Prioritize the ones you are keeping.

10. If your list is still long, take the bottom three to five and give those away as well.

Time is squishy. Value the time contribution of your people. But don't fall victim to time as a scapegoat. You can manipulate time through language choice, focus and momentum.

Chapter 12

Make Meetings Meaningful

- ● Understand Why Meetings Fail

- ● Implement the Dynamic Decision Dozen

- ● Empower Your People: The Decision Map

- ● Design Meetings to Support Decision Making

- ● Know When to Use Collaboration and When Not to Use It

- ● Apply Efficient Hand Gestures to Your Meetings

Supervisor **Co-workers** **Impact** **Autonomy** **Organizational Support**

"If you had to identify, in one word, the reason why the human race has not achieved, and never will achieve, its full potential, that word would be 'meetings.'"

—Dave Barry, author and humorist

Meetings powerful potential is often squandered. How many hours a month do you think you spend in unproductive, frustrating, boring meetings?

Now multiply:

the number of lackluster monthly meetings in your organization

×

the average number of attendees

×

the average amount of time each meeting takes

×

the average employee hourly rate

= Ouch! I know. We're not just talking about an enormous waste of time, energy and precious human contribution but also of financial resources.

Imagine what *you* could accomplish in that wasted time. Now imagine what *your team* could accomplish. When time is wasted, productivity dips. When productivity is lost, so is pride. When pride is absent, so is dignity. Meaningful meetings spark momentum, fellowship and fulfillment.

Meetings can be "weapons of mass interruption," says Al Pittampalli, author of *Read This Before Our Next Meeting*. Meetings disrupt strategic work and foster organization-wide procrastination. Pittampalli also describes how when a meeting is done well, it can be a game changing, innovative, make-your-heart-race revolutionary discussion about doing work that matters.

So when should you have a meeting? Have a meeting to...

- Make a collaborative, democratic or consensus decision.

- Debate legitimate perspectives.

- Coordinate implementation of an action plan.

- Address conflict.

- Conduct short, stand-up team coordination to quickly assess project progress and clarify next steps.

- Brainstorm solutions.

- Share bad or sensitive news.

Meetings should exist primarily to make decisions.

> "If there is nothing worth debating, we won't have a meeting."
>
> **—Patrick Lencioni,** management consultant and author

Think about it. If there is a problem to be resolved or an opportunity to consider, a meeting of the minds should answer this simple, but not always easy, question: knowing what we know, what is the best way to move forward?

Understand Why Meetings Fail

Unfortunately many meetings fail to answer this question due to:

Lack of decisiveness: The pros and cons of a decision are rehashed without coming to a conclusion. Endless discussion is not real progress; it's false progress. Teams become paralyzed by choosing the perfect option.

Choking on two cents: In an effort to make everyone feel important and included, everyone with an opinion is invited to the conversation regardless of their role.

Collaboration becomes confused with consensus: During many a meeting, I've seen leaders seek agreement, alignment, buy-in and approval from the team. The team is under the impression their opinion carries equal weight. The reality is the leader just wanted their input and suggestions and will leave the meeting and choose the best course. When the leader's decision and the team's opinion are not the same, resentment ensues.

Cowardly consensus: There is a lot of comfort and safety in collective decision making, especially if that decision fails. Safety in numbers panders to lowest common denominator solutions.

Poor facilitation: The talkers talk and the non-talkers don't. Tangents and distractions overtake the purpose of the meeting. Meetings rarely end on time.

Lack of a plan of action and follow through: A decision is made, however nobody truly owns it to champion implementation.

Sabotage and lack of in-the-room honesty: People either come to the meeting "knowing this is a waste of time" or leave the meeting murmuring to their colleagues what they "really" think, undermining the validity of the decision, causing second-guessing and disunity.

Changes to decisions aren't communicated: A decision is made in a meeting then changed in a side conversation afterwards and not communicated. This can be especially demoralizing to those who spent significant time and energy participating. They are left feeling "why'd I bother?" They also are ultimately left feeling excluded.

Static, not active: Except for rare all-company meetings where you share significant changes or important news, do not use meetings to inform. Instead use technology as a shortcut to keep everyone on the same page.

Implement the Dynamic Decision Dozen

Decisions fuel momentum and progress. If your culture suffers from chronically slow decision-making, or paralysis in choosing the right option, I recommend the following 12 questions BEFORE you call a meeting:

1. Is there a decision to be made? (If not, don't have a meeting.)

   Exceptions: If you need to create an implementation plan, address conflict, share hard news, conduct a "Cadence of Accountability" check-in, or gather to build camaraderie.

2. What is the decision that needs to be made? Clearly define it.

3. Can this be decided with one other person?

4. Who *must* be involved?

5. Who will make the decision?

   o Authoritative—I'm making the decision.*

   o Collaborative—I'm looking for help to think this through, but I will ultimately make the decision.

   o Democratic—We'll put this to a vote, and the solution with the most votes wins.

   o Consensus—We all have to agree. (Use consensus sparingly. While it's excellent for garnering buy-in, it's very time-intensive and can lead to groupthink.)

   o Delegate—You decide without me.*

   *does not require a meeting

6. What type of decision needs to be made—yes/no or choosing the best option?

7. What criteria/boundaries does the decision need to take into consideration?

8. Which of these criteria are non-negotiable vs. like to have?

9. Is this decision more important than following through on our current commitments? What will we gain?

10. What will be lost or what will we regret if we just sit on this decision?

11. How urgent is the decision? What is the finish line for the decision?

12. What does the data say? What does our gut say?

Define when it's acceptable to reopen a decision:

• If there's important new information.

• If the decision has proven not to work.

• If it's mission critical to change course.

To reopen a decision, all initial participants should gather to avoid bifurcation.

Empower Your People: The Decision Map

It's a privilege to make decisions. Decision making has creationary power. You are trusted with choosing the role and direction of limited resources. Along with this privilege, comes responsibility for the outcome.

Share this privilege and avoid a choking bottleneck. Avoid funneling every decision through one or two people. Empower people at every level to participate in creating and achieving the vision.

It's extraordinary to see your vision played out. A sense of ownership, pride and self-realization will spread throughout your organization—creating loyalty and commitment.

A Decision Map is a one-page tool empowering people at every level to know which decisions they are responsible for and have control over and which ones they don't.

Action Jackson: Questions to Consider When Creating Your Decision Map

1. How are strategic decisions about the direction of your organization made?

2. How are daily or weekly operational decisions made?

3. When is there consistency? Inconsistency?

4. Who makes what decisions? And with what permission? Who is responsible for which pieces? At the level of:

   o Ownership/Advisory Board

   o CEO/Executive Director/Dean

   o Leadership Team

   o Management Team

   o Departmental Managers

   o Front-Line Staff

5. It's not realistic to have all the decision points outlined on your map. How will you choose who the decision maker should be when unexpected questions arise?

Sample Decision Map

Board decisions

- Governance: Anything pertaining to ownership.
- Greenback Gravy: Major decisions concerning financial viability.

Leadership decisions (team ideas/suggestions/input welcomed)

- Master Plan: Strategy.
- Big Picture 3Ps: Creating or changing procedures, processes, policies.
- Promises: Contracts with clients.
- Price Tags: Pricing and sharing of pricing.
- Protection Advocacy: Safety.
- Partnerships: Vendor selection and contracts.
- Paragon Reputation: Organizational identity or brand.

Management decisions that require approval from Leadership

- Beyond the Border: Impacts more than just your department.
- Beyond the Budget: Require more than what's budgeted.
- Bring In or Move Beyond: Hiring and firing for your department.

Management decisions

- Local Picture 3Ps: Creating or changing procedures, processes, and policies specific to your department.
- Local Budget: Decisions within the scope of the budget.
- Local Success Support: Coaching team members.

Team Member decisions requiring Management approval

- Local Betterment: Modifications to procedures or processes.
- Beyond Your Bench: Impacts more than just your position.
- Beyond the Budget or the Border: Complex client issues that cost more than $XX or significantly impact another department.

Team Member decisions

- Bench Betterment: Take initiative to make the position the most effective and efficient it can be.
- Client Betterment: Take care of client issues.
- Project Betterment: Steps to make progress on a project under your purview.

Design Meetings to Support Decision Making

Create cultural context and expectations for meetings. Negative cultural underpinnings can undermine every effort to have an effective meeting. Before you have another meeting, have your entire team agree to these meeting commitments:

- Be on time—this honors all of those involved.

- Read *and digest* supporting documentation prior to the meeting. Don't just skim.

- Be curious and fully present. Listen and contribute.

- Be open to the idea the meeting will unearth better ideas and solutions than you expect.

- Say what is. Express your concerns and questions IN the meeting, not after.

- Offer kind, candid, concise and constructive communication.

- Be committed to reaching an outcome that is best for the organization.

- Be solution and progress oriented. If it's 85 percent correct and there's no mission critical concerns, back the decision. The decision doesn't have to be perfect and nitpicking or micromanaging the details is exhausting and unproductive.

- Don't be political. "Politics is when people choose their words and actions based on how they want others to react rather than based on what they really think."—Patrick Lencioni

- Do NOT bully, manipulate, ramble, blame, stall or attack.

- Acknowledge decisions are adjustable as new information is provided.

- Only commit to action items and timelines you will follow through on.

- Leave aligned. Once the decision is made, support it.

Only invite those who need to be there. Evaluate who must be involved instead of who wants to or would be nice to include.

> "Only the minimum number of people should participate. Don't invite anyone for political reasons. Don't invite anyone to socialize them on the solution because they were part of inventing it—people don't need to be in the kitchen to enjoy the meal at the restaurant."
>
> **Seth Godin,** author and entrepreneur

When you think about who needs to be in the room, think about whose help you must have:

- The decision-maker.
- Those with key knowledge or expertise.
- Manager(s) whose teams will accomplish the work or will be impacted by the decision.
- A representative from the front lines in charge of implementation.

Collect, organize and disseminate key information needed to make a well-informed decision. Include both what is known, as well as what needs to be known. This may be cost/ROI/budget, options, customer perspective, availability of resources, schedule capacity, employee feedback, team expertise, etc.

Send out the agenda along with the key information.

- Define the purpose of the meeting. What is the decision to be made or the question at hand? Clarify why it's important.
- Establish the finish line for making the decision.
- Discuss known obstacles, opportunities and potential outcomes/ solutions for the decision. Provide known pros and cons.
- Define who is the final decision maker(s).

If possible, try to have everyone meet face-to-face, in person, or virtually. So much is communicated through facial expressions and it keeps participants more present and focused.

Designate a facilitator. If you anticipate the meeting going longer than 30 minutes and including more than four people, have someone designated as the facilitator. Ideally this person is not the meeting host or decision maker who is attached to the outcome, but rather someone who can:

- Keep everyone on track and focused.*
- Pause those who dominate the conversation.
- Bring to the table those who are quieter. (I swear by using a round robin approach to hear from introverts.)
- Know when to allow the discussion to flow.
- Bring conflict safely to the surface.
- Momentarily take off the facilitator hat and contribute to the discussion.

- Hold the group accountable for accomplishing the purpose of the meeting.
- Call timing for the decision.
- End the meeting on time.

*Always have a Parking Lot. My parking lot is a flip chart to jot tangents, digressions and detours, notions that are captured but not considered. This acknowledges to your colleagues, in black and white for all to see, their contribution was heard and won't be forgotten. It also communicates that while possibly important, this topic is not critical for *this* discussion and can be addressed in another forum. For virtual teams, consider using your IM window and note PL prior to the item.

Uncover new information. Has new information arisen since the agenda was sent out?

Focus on collaboration NOT consensus. The purpose of most meetings is to choose the best option for moving forward, not to have everyone agree. However, many groups avoid conflict by seeking consensus. Critical evaluation of alternative ideas or viewpoints gets neglected, resulting in groupthink. There should be one person who is responsible for evaluating all of the input, feedback, questions, and concerns and making the final call. This person should state why they chose the option at hand and acknowledge the concerns voiced about this selection. This communicates to those who wouldn't have chosen this option their input was both heard and considered.

Make real progress. Nothing is more frustrating than a meeting that wastes everyone's time, one in which there is no discernable headway. Whenever possible, conclude with a decision. Remember, the second best solution implemented is better than the best solution not implemented. If a decision needs more research, evaluation or time to marinate, nail down how many days are needed and schedule a decision finish line meeting.

Capture and share critical outcomes. At the meeting, record the decision, the next steps and who is accomplishing which steps by when.

Confirm everyone in attendance agrees these are the outcomes of the meeting. Designate someone to provide this summary to anyone who is impacted by the decision.

Once the decision is made and next steps are in place, end the meeting.

Hold one another accountable for commitments. If items are falling through the cracks, have a direct check-in conversation with the person in charge of that item and see what support they need to make progress.

Know When to Use Collaboration and When Not to Use It

Collaboration is all the rage—for good reason. It creates a meeting of the minds, buy-in from those sitting at the table and an opportunity to consider diverse perspectives and options that may yield the best next step. However collaboration is not a cure-all. More cooks in the kitchen doesn't always make the sauce better. It can be time-consuming, inefficient and, depending on how it's facilitated, result in groupthink. Here's when to use it and when not to use it:

When to use it:

- To find a solution to a challenging ongoing issue.
- To consider the pros and cons of moving forward on an opportunity.
- At the beginning of a project to define scope, roles, goals, timeline, and desired results.
- When you want input, ideas, suggestions and feedback from multiple departments to address an issue that's central to the viability of the organization.
- To do big-picture thinking or consider major changes to the organization such as identity, service/product mix, expansion, loss of a key client, overhaul of processes.

When not to use it:

- To seek agreement or approval on a decision that's already been made.
- For non-negotiable topics.
- To discuss safety issues.
- To explore ethics.
- For decisions that require urgent action.
- For financial issues that are critical to the viability of the company.
- When working out the details of implementation. Instead, have one to three people propose a plan of action and seek input on the viability of the plan.
- For small decisions.

Action Jackson: Apply Efficient Hand Gestures to Your Meetings

No, not the middle finger. I learned about the innovative use of hand gestures in meeting facilitation a few years ago when I met Cole Wirpel, who was then President of AIESEC, the world's largest youth-run organization developing high potential youth into globally-minded leaders. Wirpel shared with me the various gestures they used in meetings to cross language barriers and communicate effectively, respectfully and efficiently:

- Thumbs up—I agree.

- Holding up a number of fingers to show where you are in line—I'd like to speak and recognize I'm after her.

- Making a wave or hilly movement—I was going to say something, but I'm good now.

- A "T" like timeout—we're going on a tangent.

- Thumb up, down, sideways—agree, disagree and block or neutral.

- Index finger twirl—wrap it up.

Think about how you could use these gestures—or create your own—in your next meeting to clearly and quickly communicate.

Let's review. Conventional meetings are both a time suck and a joykill. Team discourse is most relevant when a thoughtful decision concludes collective debate, questioning and discovery. Redesign your gatherings so they infuse energy, not apathy, into the organization. And then enjoy giving someone the twirl finger.

Chapter 13

Implement Meaningful Performance Reviews— The Triad

- Overall Best Practices

- Try The Triad of
  - The Duo Review
  - The Character and Competency Review
  - The High Five (Implement a Different 360)

| Supervisor | Meaning/ Job Fit | Autonomy | Impact | Organizational Support |

"An ounce of performance is worth pounds of promises."

—Mae West, actress, singer and provocateur

There's a movement afoot to end formal performance reviews. It's understandable. Managers and employees hate reviews. "Old school" reviews feel forced and awkward. The air is laced with the tension of condescending judgment or the useless fluff of euphemisms.

However, I am not a part of that movement. There's still value in a formal, dedicated, thoughtful time to have a real deal conversation regarding your work relationship, big picture progress and opportunities for growth. It's also a designated chance to show you care and have someone feel like they are known and that their work matters. When done well reviews are an opportunity for clarity and connection, an exchange both the manager and the employee can look forward to.

Try using The Triad, which consists of the Duo-Review, the Character and Competency Review and the High Five. I recommend conducting all three of these in a year, with a rotation of one every four months. Before I outline these, let's talk overall best practices.

Overall Best Practices

Do not talk about compensation. Separate the compensation conversation from the review. When a review includes compensation you have the Charlie Brown teacher effect: the employee doesn't hear a word until you show them the money. In addition, an employee will never challenge your constructive feedback when a raise is on the line, hence it's not really an open, honest conversation.

Do not wait until a review to address ugly issues. These issues should be dealt with as soon as possible. There should be no surprises. Reviews don't work when managers lean on them to provide feedback. Celebration of success and communication of concern must be timely.

Conduct reviews when you say you will conduct them. Integrity is critical. Not adhering to the review schedule is hypocritical. Schedule reviews. Keep that time sacred. **Or better yet, have employees be in charge** and responsible for leading the process and scheduling their reviews.

Be careful if you use scales. While tempting, I caution against using scales to measure people. You know who's working out well and who's not. You don't need a number. From the employee's perspective, to have their hard work summarized on a scale of 1–5 can be demeaning. I've also been the manager who struggled to decide if someone deserves a three or four on a given scale that has a description of "Gets along well with others." (Insert eye roll here.) Never mind grade inflation can haunt you in an unemployment case. A number alone doesn't say much. **On the flipside, meaningful scales can be useful when seeking to be objective in comparing employees.** See the Character and Competency performance review as an example.

Be fully present. Do not be late, distracted or rushed.

Provide specific examples. Whether you are giving positive or constructive feedback, make sure to provide concrete examples. This not only tells the employee you've witnessed their efforts and mishaps, you've also remembered them. It shows you care. It also helps the employee ground the feedback in something tangible they can replicate if positive or correct if constructive.

Don't sugarcoat the tough stuff. Do appreciate those efforts and behaviors you want to encourage. Don't offer the confusing sandwich of good, bad, good. It is your obligation to communicate if something is job threatening. While this should have been communicated before the review, now is the time to repeat it if it's still germane. Don't forget, your team member is likely looking for your approval; make sure to emphasize what you appreciate about them and their work.

Hold the review in a neutral space. Not in your office—perhaps in a conference room or during a walk, or at lunch or coffee outside of the office. If you have a particularly sticky topic to address meet somewhere private.

Keep it short and simple. A review should never consist of more than two pages, nor should it take more than 40 minutes.

The Duo-Review

The purpose of the duo-review is to learn from one another a) what you appreciate about each other and b) what each of you can improve upon to create a better workplace. This simultaneous assessment of both the manager and the employee allows for a more vulnerable and thus more meaningful conversation.

Because the manager has the power to hire and fire, equal vulnerability doesn't exist, **hence the openness of the manager to hear constructive feedback is critical to the success of this process.**

Both the manager and the team member should fill out the Duo-Review form (following page) prior to meeting.

At the meeting:

- Share what you appreciate about one another.

- Share *up to* three areas where the other person could improve or grow.

- Tell one another what you heard on both counts.

- Appreciate thoughtfulness and candor.

- Ask questions to uncover what specific shifts may be needed.

- Review progress on quarterly goals.

- Speak to what each of you is committed to in the next six months to expand what's working and improve in the suggested areas.

Duo Review Form

Today's Date: _____ Manager Name:_____

Team Member Name: _____

Purpose & Intention: to learn from one another what you appreciate and what you can improve upon in order to create a better relationship and more success in the workplace.

- Both the Supervisor and Employee should have a copy to fill out
- 40 minutes of scheduled **uninterrupted** time in a quiet space
- Bring a copy of the last review

A. Appreciation—what's working

1. What the Manager appreciates about the Team Member:

_____

_____

_____

2. What the Team Member appreciates about the Manager:

_____

_____

_____

B. Opportunities for Improvement—what could work better

1. What the Team Member could improve on:

_____

_____

_____

2. What the Manager could improve on:

_____

_____

_____

C. Get real and get candid: Are there any major concerns/elephants in the room we're not addressing/talking about?

_____

_____

_____

D. Look at progress on prior commitments from last review—on target?, behind?, change in priorities?

_____

_____

_____

E. Three commitments/goals for next six months:
   1. Manager:

_____

_____

_____

   2. Team Member:

_____

_____

_____

The Character and Competency Review

This review came from working with Green Ride, an award-winning airport shuttle service, who was excited to share profits with their team for the first time. They wanted this experience to be fair and to reinforce company values. Each piece of this review was intentional and tested—including the scale. This review is set up as a scorecard.

The review proved to be a method not only to determine profit portions, it also gave team members clear benchmarks to reach. Clear expectations about what it meant to be successful led employees to shift their behaviors, attitudes and performance to align with the scorecard.

This scorecard measures two aspects: exemplification of the organization's values and position performance. Customize this review to reflect the living values of your organization and the skills and expertise needed for each position. The values portion should be the same for all positions. If some performance criteria are more important, weigh them more heavily. Decide what percentage of the review will be weighted towards values and what percentage will be weighted towards performance. Make sure you have tangible examples of excellence for each value and position criteria. Add other areas of evaluation that are important for your organization, while still keeping it simple. Green Ride added "Attendance" as a metric in which an employee could only receive negative points and "Additional Contribution" in which an employee could only receive bonus points for going above and beyond. Lastly, decide if tenure will have a role in scoring.

Then test your scorecard. Run several employees through, including high, medium and low performers. Does the score accurately reflect the difference between them? Or do you need to adjust?

Character and Competency Review Example

Date: _____ Employee Name: _____

Position: _____

Manager Name: _____

Hire Date: _____

A. Exhibits Our Culture and Values (24 total points possible, 60 percent)

[Note: Your values would be listed below]

Evaluate:

Exemplary-3; Meeting Expectations-2; Needs Improvement-1; Unacceptable-0

1. **Pleasant and Professional**
   Customers like him/her and know s/he is trustworthy   _____

2. **Calm "under fire"**
   Handles problems and stressful situations thoughtfully
   Never ever reacts with anger or aggression   _____

3. **Honest**
   Admits mistakes and earns respect
   Contributes ideas and concerns for the business   _____

4. **Passionate**
   Deeply cares for customers and their challenges
   Committed to everyone's success   _____

5. **"Can do" attitude**
   Solves customer problems, takes ownership
   Takes initiative, create solutions to business challenges
   Is flexible and wears many hats   _____

6. **Responsibility**
   Owns the outcome of his/her work
   Owns the outcome of the team's work   _____

7. **Team player**
   Shares openly
   Willing to teach and help
   Great listener   _____

8. **Learning**
   Learning more skills   _____
   Professional development, education or intentional
   learning that's transferable to or benefits our organization

                                                                         Total:

                              Divide total by 24 and multiply by .60

Comments:

B. Skills/Knowledge/Capacity (24 total points possible, 40 percent)

[*Note: Your skills by role would be listed below*]

Evaluate:

Exemplary-3, Meeting Expectations-2, Needs Improvement-1, Unacceptable-0

1. **Internal Communication** _____ × 2 _____

   Respectful

   Accurate

   Timely

   Professional

2. **Complex Problem Solving** _____ × 2 _____

   Situational awareness

   Change management

3. **Plan Optimization** _____ × 2 _____

   Resource management

   Efficient routing

   Planning accuracy

   Attention to detail

4. **Role Versatility** _____

5. **Tool Knowledge and Efficiency** _____

   Total:

   Divide total by 24 and multiply by .40

C. Attendance

(3 absences or less = 0, 4 absences = –1, 5 absences = –5, 6 absences = –10)

- Less than 24 hours notice constitutes an absence
- Includes mandatory meetings
- 3 absences/year allowed   –

D. Additional Contribution:

(Bonus—up to ten possible additional points)

- Creates and implements projects or initiatives
- Goes above and beyond consistently
- Pushes the envelope of our company to make us better   +

Total (add up all gray sections):

Implement a Different 360

This is the third leg of the triad. I struggle with traditional 360 reviews because they formalize indirect communication on their best days and encourage passive aggressive communication on their worst. Also, if they're truly anonymous, who knows what was meant by "needs to improve communication." If they are anonymous to the employee, but not to the manager, the manager has to follow up with the feedback giver and find out what was meant by "needs to improve communication" and then find a way to couch it so it's not obvious who said it. If they are anonymous to the employee and to the manager, but not the consultant, then the consultant charges you for their time to find the answer and couch it. With 360s you have two options: couching or lack of clarity. Both stink. Both are ineffective and a significant time suck.

Yet peer feedback that helps a co-worker see their blind spots is gold. What do you do?

Solution: The High Five

Once a year, have every employee, leadership included, select five co-workers from whom they think feedback would be the most valuable. It is then the employee's responsibility to set up 15-minute one-on-ones with each of these five co-workers. The employee asks the following five questions.

What is the one thing:

1. You appreciate most about me as a co-worker?
2. I could do to be a better co-worker?
3. You think I rock at in my position?
4. I could do (or learn) to be better at my job?
5. I could do to help you be successful?

The employee can then directly ask for clarity, through examples as well as suggestions. This helps the person learn not only what to improve, but how. Because everyone participates in this process, everyone is more committed to being both humble and open to receiving input as well as courageous and kind in their feedback. The employee brings the feedback, insights and suggestions they receive to a dialogue with their manager to talk through next steps.

To make this process successful, train your team on the Five Success Factors of the giver and the receiver:

As the Feedback Giver:

1. **Show up on time.**

2. **Show up as a stand for the individual's success.** Your intentions will make all the difference in how your feedback is perceived and received.

3. **Be kind, candid and constructive.** Don't couch your communication. Don't be harsh.

4. **Don't phone it in.** Say something meaningful. Take time beforehand to think through what you want to convey. Come prepared with examples and suggestions.

5. **Start off with a humble qualifying statement.**

   o From my perspective...

   o In my experience working with you...

   o I may be missing something, however it would seem...

As a Feedback Receiver:

1. **Trust the givers' intentions.** They are there to help you be the best you can be—not to criticize or judge.

2. **Be curious, not defensive.** Stay present and seek to understand. Ask questions. (Sometimes you just need to take it in and sleep on it.)

3. **Be thankful for all suggestions.** Appreciate the courage it took for the other person to share their perspective and be straight with you.

4. **You don't have to take "on" all suggestions.** They may not all be accurate. Those that are repeated hold more weight.

5. **Lastly, don't get stuck in your head!** Instead make progress.

There's still a place for thoughtfully crafted performance reviews that spur meaningful exchanges. Take the time. Don't phone it in. Don't miss out on this guaranteed chance to demonstrate you care. The alignment alone will come back to you fivefold and strengthen the relationship.

Chapter 14

Crack the Compensation Code

- Mitigate Money Stories

- Beware Toxic Culture Red Flag

- Compensate for Value and Versatility

- Bandwidth Compensation to Value Your Best Producers

- Decide How Compensation is Determined

- Avoid Extortion and Support Those Who Want to Leave

- Define How Raises are Determined

- Choose Compensation Package Options

- Beware Profit Sharing, Bonuses, Commissions and Incentives

| Supervisor | Coworkers | Organizational Support | Organizational Fit |

"Price is what you pay. Value is what you get."

—Warren Buffett, investor and business magnate

How much am I worth to you?

That's a tough question for anyone to answer. It's incredibly personal. There's no dollar number that *feels* right in response. You can't put a price on a person. You aren't paying for that person. You're paying for the value they bring to the organization through their work. However, many employees collapse these two. In this chapter I'll recommend how to navigate the choppy waters of compensation.

Mitigate Money Stories

While money is fictitious paper, its reality as energy is undeniable. It empowers Maslow's hierarchy of needs: physiological, safety, love and belonging, esteem and self-actualization. Money spurs self-determination and autonomy. It provides a roof over our heads and food in our bellies. Money nurtures security, health and well-being. It expands generosity, nourishes dreams and personal missions.

Money is emotional. By association, compensation is emotional. Keep in mind, every individual has a money story through which they filter their compensation.

Here are just a few common money stories:

- Money is the root of all evil.
- Money doesn't grow on trees.
- The best things in life are free.
- I can't hold on to money.
- There's never enough money.
- To want money is greedy.
- There's more of where that came from.

While you can't control these stories, under the umbrella of career development and financial literacy, you can suggest thoughtful consideration of these questions to create self-awareness:

1. What was your childhood experience of money? How did your parents handle money? What did they tell you about money? What was modeled for you? What money messages did you receive?

2. What are your beliefs and thoughts about money? What do you assume about people who have money? What do you assume about people who don't? What do you believe about your current financial situation?

3. What words do you associate with money? What do you say to your kids or to your friends about money? What advice do you give?

4. What are your habits and actions around money?

5. Of these beliefs, words and habits, which serve you? Which don't?

6. How do you define financial freedom?

When an employee understands their default money framework, it allows them to actively choose a different one. *Especially if they take compensation as a concrete measurement of their worth.* One of the best benefits you can provide any team is personal financial literacy and mastery training. Find a good non-profit resource. Don't lean on your benefits provider, mutual funds investor, banker or anyone who would seek to sell your team a financial product or service.

 Favorite Resource: If you're a manager who would like to improve your own business financial literacy, I highly recommend *Financial Intelligence* by Karen Berman and Joe Knight.

Also consider, for some, psychological compensation is as strong as monetary compensation. Flexibility, alignment of values, appreciation, daily joy and humor, and camaraderie figure heavily in how an employee determines the value of working for you.

Lastly, know employees will naturally share their money stories with their colleagues. Whatever you do, don't discourage employees from sharing their pay with one another. It suggests you have something to hide or that the system is not fair. Your employees *will* talk to one another. By trying to suppress those conversations you will undermine your culture.

While you can't shape their money stories, you can control how your organization defines value, the process by which compensation is determined and how raises are given.

Beware Toxic Culture Red Flag

Note, if you commonly have employees asking for a raise who haven't done anything to earn it, or who just recently received a raise, they may be telling you the psychological compensation isn't sufficient.

They are asking you to make it worthwhile to put up with:

- Insane inefficiencies and lack of communication.

- The rude supervisor.

- The inept co-worker who should have been fired long ago.

- Irate customers to whom organizational promises are continuously broken.

Imagine your employee goes home after yet another frustrating day of work and again kvetches to their spouse about the dysfunctional culture. The spouse pounds their fist on the table, "Honey, you shouldn't have to put up with that BS! They don't know how much you're worth! You march right into your boss's office tomorrow and demand a raise!"

If someone is not happy with the culture, it doesn't really matter how much you pay. It won't be worth it. It won't be enough. This will become obvious when they leave even after you give them an unreasonable raise.

Compensate for Value and Versatility

Pay for skills that bring value to the organization. We all have one person on our team who can pinch hit in multiple positions. They are your Swiss Army knife. Pay them as such. When I ran the moving company, the movers had a clear way of improving their pay based on advancing their skillset, versatility and value to the company. The more versatile an employee was, the more valuable they were to our organization. Keep in mind these wages reflect those of 2007.

- No moving experience, non-driver: $10/hour

- Minimum of 6 months of moving experience: +$1

- Able to drive and complete an accurate pre-trip: +$1

- Able to pack: +$1

- Able to lead a crew: +$1
- Able to train on the above: +$1
- Able to drive a Class B CDL truck: +$1
- Able to drive a Class A CDL truck: +$1
- Able to run national moves: day rates significantly higher

I required six months between each raise unless we were in dire need of that skill. Then I waived the waiting period. I asked my most talented movers to create demonstrable expectations for each skill. Skill achievement was evaluated by peer experts. Raises also were dependent on attitude and values exemplification. If you had a negative attitude, regardless of skill achievement, you didn't get a raise.

This accomplished several key cultural norms:

- Transparency. Everyone knew what everyone else was making based on their versatility and attitude.
- A feeling of fairness when comparing yourself to peers.
- Clear expectations. Movers knew they could make anywhere from $10–$17/hour, which is what we could afford. Once someone hit the ceiling, it was clear they would not get a raise for some time. It was economics, not a lack of appreciation.
- A sense of ownership and pride by the more experienced crew of mentoring the upcoming crew.
- An interest in learning the profession, progressing and becoming more masterful.
- Less competition and more camaraderie. Your raise wasn't dependent on someone else not getting theirs.

You may have a more complex organization with many departments. Still, know your employees are comparing themselves most within their own departments, within their team. You can create this same paradigm within each department.

For those of you whose organizations have lower-wage employees, consider comparing your compensation to MIT's Living Wage Calculator for meeting basic needs: http://livingwage.mit.edu/.

Bandwidth Compensation to Value Your Best Producers

"Create heroes in every role. Make every role, performed at excellence, a respected profession," Marcus Buckingham and Curt Coffman from their book *First, Break All the Rules.* "If a company wants some employees in every role to approach world-class performance, *it must find* ways to encourage them to stay focused on developing their expertise. Defining graded levels of achievement for every role is an extremely effective way of doing just that."

We created levels of achievement in the mover/driver role. Buckingham and Coffman took this one step further with the concept of bandwidthing. With bandwidthing, each role has a range of compensation *and* the **top of one range is higher than the bottom of the next range.**

For example, your best housekeeper would make more than the new housekeeping manager. To be promoted to another role means accepting a pay cut since they would start out at the bottom of the range, though the long-term financial potential would be higher. An employee would have to be truly committed to the new position, rather than just applying to gain prestige or additional compensation. This also helps you avoid taking your best producer and prematurely promoting them.

Bandwidthing values, honors, and appreciates the mastery, wisdom and proficiency of your most talented staff in every position.

Decide How Compensation is Determined

First, determine what you're going to pay for each position, rather than a specific employee.

- What value does this position bring to the organization?
- How hard is it to find employees with these skills in the marketplace?
- What wage would be competitive in our marketplace?
- What wage can we afford when evaluating costing and profitability?
- What wage would reflect our values?
- What is the range of compensation for this position?

Second, decide how much you're going to pay a particular employee.

- What is the value of the specific expertise, skills and relationships this individual brings to the organization?
- How productive is this individual?
- How well does this person exemplify the values of our organization? How much do they contribute to creating an extraordinary workplace culture? Remember there's a huge ROI

for having happy employees. Influencers who help create an empowering context for their co-workers bring additional value.

What about seniority? Compensation packages should reflect performance, versatility and contribution rather than tenure. I honor loyalty and years of service through anniversary celebrations. Consider providing a universal gift for each year of service. For example, one company gives employees with two years of service a plane ticket to anywhere in the United States. After three years, it gives them two plane tickets. After four years, the reward is a ticket to anywhere in the world. After five years, it's two international tickets.

The purpose of a compensation package is to define fair reciprocity for a job well done. Culture deteriorates when compensation is used to manipulate. Exceptions get made and along with them come disastrous cultural implications.

Common exceptions:

- Paying more to recruit new employees for the same position level.

- Paying more to keep an employee who threatens to leave.

- Paying more to motivate an employee to work harder.

Paying more is not the problem. The problem is paying more to a single individual for no discernable reason. If you can justify paying one person more, then you need to increase pay for those in the same position with similar responsibilities, versatility, values exemplification and results. If you're not going to pay similarly, you have to explain why.

When you pay more, you say what you value. You put your money where your mouth is. In these instances, you value new people more than you do your loyal veterans. You value extortion. You value underperformers. Whenever you choose to pay someone more than their peers, think—really think—about the implications.

Avoid Extortion and Support Those Who Want to Leave

Create a new cultural norm by both requesting and making it safe for employees to communicate if they are unhappy with their job or compensation *prior* to looking for other work. If an employee does not give you this courtesy, *and* has sought other employment and is so far down the path as to have an offer to leverage, let them go. They don't really want to work for your organization. Golden handcuffs are still handcuffs.

I do want to acknowledge that traditionally if someone wants to leave your organization, they don't tell you. They look for a job, secure one, and then provide two weeks' notice—leaving you to scramble to find and train their replacement. Transition becomes a fire drill.

Employees don't share their desire to leave with the intention of causing their employers strife. They don't tell their employers for fear of getting fired. I've literally heard a manager say, "Well if you don't want to be here, don't let the door hit you on the way out." What a cluster.

I had the amazing opportunity of having Christie Naus, my right hand communications coordinator, on our team for more than two and a half years. I knew early on she would grow beyond Choose People. "When you're ready to transition, please let me know before you start looking for another position," I told her when she was hired. She did.

She shared with me her desire to be part of a larger work community (we're a small team) and to be in an organization where she would have opportunities to advance as well as have full benefits. She said she hadn't started looking yet. I was deeply honored by both her thoughtfulness and her courage in sharing her desire to find her next career opportunity.

Which left me with only one choice—to help her!

She received support and encouragement in finding her next opportunity. I received support in completing key work projects and training her replacement.

However here's what's even better—she found her replacement. You know how you spend all that time and energy to find someone who's the right fit? Because Christie was truly committed to our mission, and knew what the position required as well as my management style and our culture, she thought about who would rock the role.

So let me ask you, if you don't already know, what would it look like to genuinely support someone who wanted to leave? It's a radical notion. Perhaps you would forward their resume to your colleagues, make a recommendation on their LinkedIn account, be their wing woman at a networking event, or write a blog post to support them in finding a position that would leverage their brilliance in the world.

Define How Raises are Determined

Raises should be entwined with the performance results of the individual, the team and the organization. The organization has to be

financially healthy before doling out raises. When sharing the financials or the strategic plan, define what it means for the organization to be financially healthy. What revenue and profit numbers have to be achieved?

Second, an employee needs to increase their value to the organization by being more versatile, producing more revenue, reducing costs or producing better results. In essence, an employee needs to increase their return on investment.

Don Phin of HRthatWorks recommends telling employees, "Do not request a raise simply because you need more money. We regularly provide our employees with salary or wage increases based on market surveys and consumer price indexes. All other raises are based on performance profitability only. Be prepared to explain how you've improved your performance and how it affects the company's bottom line."

Define when people should ask for raises. Any time? Certain times of the year? Can they be on a performance improvement plan? Is there a "waiting" period between raises?

Choose Compensation Package Options

There are many creative ways to put together a compensation package. Consider these monetary, non-monetary, direct and indirect options:

Monetary

- Hourly wage, overtime, salary
- Performance based pay: commissions or bonuses
- Profit sharing

Direct Benefits

- Vacation
- Personal days, sick days
- Health insurance—medical, dental, vision
- Disability insurance, life insurance
- Paid parental leave

- Employee assistance program
- 401K contributions
- Equity/stock options

Indirect Monetary Benefits

- Tips
- Gym, gym membership, race fees, yoga class, Fitbits
- Rideshare, mileage reimbursement
- Cell phone payment
- Career development—pay for training or education
- Childcare
- Lunch, breakfast, Friday afternoon club
- Tickets to a game or concert
- Laundry service, dry cleaning service, housekeeping
- Magazine subscription
- Team sponsorship

Indirect Non-Monetary Benefits

- Emotionally healthy workplace—great culture ☺
- Flexible schedule
- Job security
- Praise and recognition
- Opportunity for growth
- Mentorship
- Task enjoyment—new types of projects or work
- Friendships, co-worker camaraderie
- Time to learn or pursue a creative work-related project
- Meditation or nap room
- Pride working for your organization
- Formal fun gatherings
- Real cream and soft toilet paper
- Inspiring workspace

- Windows or good lighting
- Quality tools
- Support of an outside talent or interest—their baseball game, play, poetry slam

Beware of Profit Sharing, Bonuses, Commissions and Incentives

I've had many leaders ask me about various ways of connecting compensation and performance. The intention to motivate and reward great performance as well as share the wealth seems reasonable and generous. Often, though, these intentions pave the road to tension, broken promises, frustration and entitlement.

First and foremost, a financially healthy organization that can cover its payroll with ease, pay its vendors on time, have low to no debt, is able to invest in small niceties and have six months of expenses in the bank is more important to your culture than the short-term morale bump of any of these options.

Second, if people are paid well and fairly, and you have an extraordinary workplace culture, they don't need carrots. They will work hard for you because they care and they know you care.

Third, do not try to fix your culture challenges by throwing money at your team. It doesn't work. The elephants will still be there tomorrow, wearing a new jewel encrusted tiara.

Prudent Profit Sharing

While I love the idea of profit sharing because it truly shares the wealth, it has significant challenges:

- Annual profit sharing doesn't address sharing the struggle in down years nor playing catch up from those same years.
- Cash flow can be very different from profit, causing a cash crunch.
- Employees may want to delay long term growth investment choices in resources such as new staff, software, equipment etc. if they think it will impact this year's profit.

- If you are growing quickly, you need cash for capital investments to increase capacity.

- You can have a great year revenue-wise and meet revenue goals, and still not have the profit and cash you need to do profit sharing.

Unexpected Bonuses

Here are my recommendations as far as bonuses:

- Do not include bonuses in compensation packages.

- Bonuses should not be an expected part of your employee's personal budget for income.

- Do not leverage bonuses as an incentive.

- Do not insinuate a bonus is coming.

- Instead use bonuses as an unexpected thank you.

- Distribute bonuses randomly rather than creating expectation and entitlement. Specifically, don't bonus at the holidays. Bonuses should be based on unexpected financial success, not the time of year. (Many organizations look to dump cash for tax purposes at the end of the year; reconsider this strategy.)

- Have it be understood, "We did well this quarter and I wanted to share the wealth you helped create. Thank you for your continued hard work and efforts."

- Consider smaller bonuses more often.

- Consider non-cash bonuses: half-day off, catered lunch, mariachi band to serenade the team, two-hour coupon for house cleaning, tickets for everyone to a local game.

- Bonuses should reflect team effort and organizational success rather than individual achievement.

Commission Caution

Commissions are different from incentives. An incentive prods a team member into accomplishing an optional task, while a commission pays for performance on a task that is directly part of their duties. If you're going to pay commissions, first make them departmental team based to deepen peer pressure and peer support. After all, the team as a whole needs to perform well to be successful. Second, commissions only work when you can easily and clearly measure how they are awarded:

- Number of orders shipped (warehouse)
- Number of new clients (marketing)
- Number of retained clients (account managers)
- Percentage of A/R received (accounts receivable)
- Hitting a project finish line (engineering)
- Positive customer feedback (customer service)

But here's the kicker and the reason commissions make me nervous: the team has to feel they have full domain over the factors that impact the number being measured. There can be no gray. Otherwise you can end up with finger pointing animosity.

Incentives

The problem with most incentive programs is they're condescending. The typical program looks like, "If we complete ten orders, everyone will get a new iPad."

To suggest the reason your team works hard is to receive a prize, rather than because of their inherent work ethic, is demeaning. My movers weren't working hard and going the extra mile for pizza. They were working to feed their families and to help people make it through one of the most difficult transitions in their life.

If the desired efforts and outcomes are tied to supporting the mission, then your team's hard work, loyalty and commitment are "priceless." To exchange it for a tchotchke cheapens the effort and robs the team of the intrinsic warm fuzzy pride they receive in simply being the best they can be because they care.

 Favorite Resource: In *Drive: The Surprising Truth about What Motivates Us,* Daniel Pink notes the richest experiences in our lives come from "doing something that matters, doing it well and doing it in the service of a cause larger than ourselves." Incentives, he points out, suggest the work is so undesirable you have to manipulate employees to do it.

Compensation that aligns with the value brought to the organization by each person is compensation that upholds an extraordinary culture. It's transparent, it's fair and there's not a whiff of manipulation.

How much am I worth to you? You are invaluable. I cannot pay for you. I can only pay for your contribution.

Conclusion

I cleaned toilets. I swabbed cat pee from the pantry where the little monster snuck in the night before. I washed out maggot-laden trashcans. I scrubbed trays and trays of baked-on BBQ pans. I also weed-wacked, waitressed and helped with the horses at a dude ranch in Moab, Utah for three summers. I was paid primarily in room and board. I was 16.

I loved it. I loved the woman I worked for and I loved the people I worked with. I loved the challenge, the variety, the autonomy and the clear and regular feedback. I always knew where I stood. I knew how I could improve. I also knew why this ranch existed, and what we as a team were up to creating for our guests—a desert paradise, a sanctuary.

Most people don't mind working hard.

In fact, they prefer it. There's tremendous self-satisfaction in a job well done. It feels good when the end of the day arrives and you've made real progress. You've earned your keep, and then some.

It feels even better when you believe in what your organization is creating in the world, and you value making that vision a reality. You have clarity of what you need to make happen each day. You not only feel joy in the workplace, you have a sense of pride.

Someone acknowledges your contribution. Add being a stand for your success and supporting your growth, and the magic starts to stir. Throw in feeling like you really belong and genuinely connect with your co-workers, and a bunny pops out of a top hat.

Your leaders make the tough choices. Jerks get fired, and underperformers earn a chance.

Gossip isn't an issue. It's safe to say what needs to be said. You can admit to mistakes and bring up concerns. Your suggestions are heard, considered and answered. How the organization makes, saves and spends money is shared.

An extraordinary workplace culture feels like magic. But it's not magic. There is an intentional plan, a trusted recipe. You just follow it, step by step, chapter by chapter.

Remember though, once you create an extraordinary workplace culture, you can't just set it and forget it. It must be nurtured. Continue to use the temperature check, adhere to operationalization of your values, and throw in some speed dating. Share the financials, keep compensation fair and encourage Funkytown conversations. Always keep on hand the secret ingredient of emotional intimacy.

Remember, your team is a reflection of you. So regularly ask yourself, do I feel joy when I walk into my workplace?

Apply and Continue the Learning

First, if you haven't already, go to www.choosepeople.com and sign up for our free weekly Culture Tip.

Second, this book is intentionally a how-to book, meaning we hope you apply what you learn!

We created the *Culture Works Workbook* and the Culture Works Book Club to support your efforts to apply this content and implement shifts to create real-deal progress. You've GOT this! We're just here to keep the momentum rolling and the inspiration rockin.'

We'll supply the tools for your leaders to gather together once a month to discuss how you can better lead your teams and improve your workplace culture. Read one chapter a month, try on one key concept and then come back to your colleagues to share what worked and what didn't.

Take action. Make progress. Feel great. Repeat.

I'm a stand for your success. I want you to have an extraordinary workplace culture, I want your team to feel good about coming to work, and I want your cultural foundation of happiness to not only put smiles on faces, but also bring joy to your bottom line. I know that this triad—the book, the workbook and the book club—together with your commitment will create significant shifts in improving your workplace culture.

Culture Works Workbook

The *Culture Works Workbook* gives you breathing room to think, commit, try on and reflect. It takes all of the tangible tools, Action Jacksons and questions and puts them in one place—with space. Space to write. Why the write space? We process when we write. We commit and take action when we put pen to paper. And we remember more when we write.

The workbook also includes deep dive discussion guides, sticky mini-mantras to remember key concepts, and obstacle obliterators.

Culture Works Book Club

The Culture Works Book Club fuels your forward progress. It keeps your momentum, focus and inspiration rolling. Each month you'll get:

1. New Insightful Culture Improving Content, Concepts and Case Studies (delivered in two, 3–5 minute videos)

2. One Kick Booty Culture Improving Tool—beyond what's in the book! (delivered directly to your inbox)

3. Expert Advice to Your Questions: Each month you can submit your most pressing culture questions and Kris will answer them! Answers delivered in a 45-minute live office-hours format that will be recorded, posted and transcribed.

Individual Book Club Bonus: If you share your thoughts and suggestions on the "Culture Quandary of the Month" you will receive all of the compiled responses and recommendations. And should you participate each month for a year, you will also receive our esteemed "Culture Works Certificate of Commitment."

Team Book Club Bonus: Teams of eight or more who sign up together receive a 45-minute custom Kick-Off and Q & A video call with Kris. Grill me on your most pressing culture issues!

To purchase the Culture Works Workbook and/or to sign up for the Culture Works Book Club, simply go to www.cultureworksbook.com

Return on Investment of Happy Employees Stats

1. The productivity loss of one unhappy employee who makes $65,000 is $75 per week or $3900 per year.

   Source: Thomas Wright, Jon Wefald Leadership Chair in Business Administration and Professor of Management at Kansas State University.

2. Happy workers are 12 percent more productive than average while unhappy workers are 10 percent less productive than average— for a total spread of 22 percent!

   Source: Andrew Oswald, a Professor of Economics at Warwick Business School.

3. Employees in highly participative work climates provided 14 percent better customer service, committed 26 percent fewer clinical errors, demonstrated 79 percent lower burnout, and felt 61 percent lower likelihood of leaving the organization than employees in more authoritarian work climates.

   Source: Angermeier, Dunford, Boss & Boss; *Journal of Healthcare Management.*

4. Higher workplace engagement leads to 41 percent lower absenteeism, 58 percent fewer safety incidents, and 40 percent fewer quality defects.

   Source: Gallup "The Relationship Between Engagement at Work and Organizational Outcomes" 2016 Q12® Meta Analysis: Ninth Edition.

5. Correlation between customer satisfaction and company culture is so strong that the difference in revenue between salespeople in strong and weak company cultures was 30 percent.

   Source: Lindsay McGregor and Neel Doshi, *Primed to Perform: How to Build the Highest Performing Cultures Through the Science of Total Motivation.*

6. The likelihood of job turnover at an organization with rich company culture is a mere 13.9 percent, whereas the probability of job turnover in poor company cultures is 48.4 percent."

   Source: Elizabeth Medina Columbia University study "Job Satisfaction and Employee Turnover Intention: What Does Organizational Culture Have to Do With It?"

7. High engagement and enablement improves employee performance by 50 percent, reduces employee turnover by 54 percent, increases customer satisfaction rates by 89 percent and increases five-year revenue growth by 450 percent.

   Source: KornFerry Hay Group "Real World Leadership" Global Study, 2015.

8. Workers who are on the receiving end of incivility decrease their work effort by 48 percent, quality of work by 38 percent, and commitment to the organization by 78 percent. 25 percent admitted to taking their frustration out on customers.

   Source: Professors Christine Porath and Christine Pearson "The Price of Incivility" in *Harvard Business Review*, 2013.

9. Cost of turnover is 6–9 months salary of that employee.

   Source: Society for Human Resource Management.

10. Your brain at positive is 31 percent more productive than your brain at negative, neutral or stressed. You're 37 percent better at sales.

    Source: Shawn Achor, author of *The Happiness Advantage*.

11. Research has long shown emotions are contagious.

    Source: Susan Weinschenk, Ph.D. "Emotions are Contagious" in *Psychology Today*, 2016.

12. The most important recruitment factor is workplace culture.

    Source: LinkedIn's Talent Trends 2014 report.

Acknowledgements

Thank you so much to the incredible team who diligently worked with me to get this book launched. Without you I wouldn't have made it through the fire.

With deep gratitude and appreciation, I would like to acknowledge:

My patient and supportive husband, John Conn, who didn't lose love over months of my hyper focus on this book and was willing to be my daily sounding board.

Madison Gonzalez Boesch and Aidan Levy thank you for continuing to inspire me and make me proud both of who you are and what you're up to in the world.

Maureen Boyt and Tamara Kleinberg whose advice, insight and support continues to be invaluable. Thank you for brilliantly naming this book.

Bree Allmon who has always helped me keep my inspiration rockin' and rollin' and lit the ultimate fire under me to finally get this book written.

Christie Naus and Shelley Fletcher for being amazing Choose People wing-women who held down the fort.

Jim Morrison, my editor, for whom this book reads oh so much better. Thank you for both "waiting" for the manuscript to arrive and teaching me how to have a more authoritative voice.

The extraordinary team at ToolBox Creative—special thanks to Dawn Putney, Tom Campbell, Shane Miles and Lulu Tupper for this book's beautiful interior design as well as website design and creation.

Holly White of SurveyGizmo who is not only a rock climber and fire dancer, but also programmed the Culture Assessment.

Alex Seciu who brilliantly designed all of the illustrations in this book with minimal direction.

Ivan Kurylenko who designed both the book and workbook covers and was kindly patient with all of my edits.

The Weaving Influence PR team—special thanks to Becky Robinson, Christy Kirk, Lori Weidert, Mike Driehorst and Christy Lynn Wilson.

All of my very kind, candid and constructive beta-readers—many listed above as well as **Jim Finnegan, Beth Hutchinson, Andy Fletcher and my Mom and Dad** ☺.

All of my clients who continue to inspire me with their dedication and commitment to human potential and expanding joy in their workplace.

About the Author

There is nothing more reward-ing for Kris Boesch than to help usher in powerful workplace culture transformation—to see people inspired, excited and joy-filled.

Kris Boesch is the CEO and Founder of Choose People, based in Denver, Colorado. The high-energy Choose People team is dedicated to transforming workplace cultures for organizations across the nation, with the goal to both increase employee happiness and boost the bottom line. Kris will tell you an organization's financial and emotional health are absolutely intertwined.

Kris is also a nationally renowned speaker and highly regarded culture expert. Known for her TEDxMileHigh presentation, "How to Create Emotional Intimacy in the Workplace," she may have set the world record for the largest "wave" in an opera house with more than 2,000 attendees. Kris' talks are effective, powerful and emotional experiences, intended to deeply impact and inspire audiences to take meaningful action. To view Kris' TEDxMileHigh talk along with other recent keynotes visit KrisBoesch.com.

Kris' focus on workplace culture began years ago as CEO of a regional moving company. Under her leadership the company, which was failing due to a culture of hostility and conflict, was quickly trans-formed to become the largest mover in Northern Colorado—with a turnover rate 40% less than the industry average and profits twice that same average.

After leaving the moving company, Kris started Choose People in 2010. Before opening her doors, she spent a year developing the Choose People 360 Culture Audit™. This audit is based on over one thousand hours of research. Kris collaborated with the Industrial Organizational Psychology Department at Colorado State University. By tapping into the research and applying it to real deal, real world situations Kris was able to identify trends, patterns and models that apply to nearly any workplace. As a result, she quickly produces extraordinary and long-lasting results for her clients.

Kris lives in Denver, Colorado and is a proud mother, dancing diva and dog lover.

CPSIA information can be obtained
at www.ICGtesting.com
Printed in the USA
FSOW01n1345030318
45211FS

9 780998 671123